SIMPLE
TREASURES

from the collection of
CANADIAN ROCKY MOUNTAIN RESORTS

APPETIZERS

SOUPS

SALADS

FISH

MEAT

CONTENTS

"These mountains are our temples,
our sanctuaries, and our resting places.
They are a place of hope, a place of vision, a place
of refuge, a very special and holy place where
the Great Spirit speaks with us.... These
mountains are our sacred places."

Chief John Snow, Stoney Indian Band

INTRODUCTION

We are very fortunate at Canadian Rocky Mountain Resorts (CRMR) to have a highly skilled, professional and dedicated team of chefs. Their tenure with CRMR ranges from 3 to 17 years. Our executive chef Mr. Alistair Barnes was originally retained as chef for the opening of Emerald Lake Lodge in July 1986. Cumulatively, our nine head chefs have been with CRMR for 85 years. We are extremely proud of this tenure and dedication.

Of our nine head chefs, four came into the company in the role of chef and five worked their way up through our kitchens. Four of our chefs left CRMR to further their careers and later returned. We feel honoured that they chose to return to CRMR when there were many options available to them.

Simple Treasures is a result of the initiative and drive of our executive chef Alistair Barnes. Our other chefs have all contributed to the book directly by working with Alistair on the recipes and indirectly by being dedicated to their profession. Connie, Alistair and I have been talking about producing a CRMR cookbook for years. As you can well imagine, it is a vast amount of work and takes an extraordinary amount of time. The only way that Alistair could dedicate time to this project is to have eight competent chefs run eight efficient kitchens.

Connie and I have a passion for quality food. From the outset, we had a clear vision of the cuisine we wanted our kitchens to produce. But, not being professional chefs, we could not and cannot attain our goals without chefs that share this same vision. Our group of chefs not only share this vision, they make it happen and they make it enjoyable. We are always happy when we are collaborating with our chefs.

We have now been in the resort/restaurant business for approximately 25 years. Even though it is fraught with problems and is extremely demanding, it is an industry we both love. We would like to thank our chefs for their tremendous contribution.

This book is dedicated to our head chefs:

Alistair Barnes
  Executive Chef, CRMR
Alan Bancroft
  Pastry Chef, CRMR
Linda Calabrese
  Chef, Buffalo Mountain Lodge
Ken Canavan
  Chef, Cilantro
John Donovan
  Chef, Divino
Valerie Morrison
  Chef, Emerald Lake Lodge
Thomas Neukom
  Chef, The Ranche Restaurant
Kelly Strutt
  Chef, Deer Lodge
Shane Swiss
  Chef, Velvet
David Cox
  Chef, THE RESTAURANT at Painted Boat

Pat and Connie O'Connor

It is my pleasure to welcome you to the kitchens of the Canadian Rocky Mountain Resorts. The following recipes are selected from our mountain resorts, Buffalo Mountain Lodge, Deer Lodge and Emerald Lake Lodge, and from our Calgary restaurants Divino, The Ranche, Cilantro and Velvet.

In our mountain restaurants and lodges we strive to offer guests a unique experience by combining a truly regional cuisine with locally sourced, seasonal products. Meals are served in the historic dining rooms featuring open fires, native art, hand hewn logs and beautiful natural surroundings.

Our city restaurants offer the highest standards in culinary art. Our chefs work closely with local producers which enables the chefs to incorporate the freshest ingredients into the various styles of food we offer — from French American Bistro to Regional and Southwestern cuisine.

FOREWORD

The selected recipes are a cornucopia of new and old. At some point in the last 20 years, they have all been served in our restaurants and many have been requested by diners. I have tried to keep recipes as simple as possible with easy to follow instructions and readily available ingredients, while staying true to their identity.

I first arrived in Alberta as a ambitious young chef in the spring of 1978, after learning the beginnings of my trade in Europe. I started my cook's apprenticeship on my 15th birthday at the historical Grand Hotel in Jersey, Channel Islands. This apprenticeship lasted three years. I worked 6 days a week and attended culinary school on my day off. This gave me the basic cook's title of Commis Chef, but more importantly it enabled me to pursue my profession almost anywhere in the world.

In Alberta in 1978, many products that we take for granted today — fresh herbs, game meats, heirloom fruits and vegetables — were simply not available. Fortunately, today we have a network of local farmers and specialty suppliers, including our own game farm that raises naturally grazed elk, bison and caribou, that keep our restaurants supplied with top-notch ingredients.

The hospitality business is a very rewarding but demanding profession. Our staff are often at work when other people are off — nights, weekends, holidays and summer months.

In the mountain lodges, the first cooks start their shifts at 5 a.m. and heat up the ovens, grills and flattops ready for our first guests of the day around 7 a.m. The kitchen is still buzzing at midnight, when the cooks clean their work areas, check and wrap products, and get everything ready for the next day's service.

All successful chefs are able to multi-task, are organized and creative, are able to keep staff and guests happy, and enjoy the adrenalin rush and managed stress of a hectic lunch or dinner service. It is wonderfully satisfying to have served a dining room full of happy customers.

I hope the recipes in this book will bring a piece of western Canada to your home, and perhaps inspire you to come and visit us in the wild, beautiful and majestic Canadian Rockies.

Alistair Barnes

Rocky Mountain Game Platter

APPETIZERS

Nicoise Salad with Fresh Seared Tuna

VINAIGRETTE

2 shallots, fine diced

2 tbsp red pepper, fine diced

¼ cup nicoise olives chopped, or other black olive

1 tsp minced garlic

½ tsp cardamom

1 tsp roasted fennel seed

¼ cup honey

1 lemon, juiced

¼ cup champagne vinegar

¼ cup olive oil

salt & fresh pepper

SALAD

1 cup fresh baby green beans, blanched

1 cup cherry tomatoes

1½ cups baby red potatoes, quartered and blanched

½ cup nicoise olives, or other black olive

2 hard boiled eggs, roughly chopped

1 head butter leaf lettuce, separated and washed

½ cup dressing

4 sprigs fresh basil

4 x 4 oz (125g) fresh tuna steaks

NICOISE SALAD WITH SEARED FRESH TUNA

Whisk all ingredients for the vinaigrette together, adjust seasoning as required.

Season tuna with fresh ground pepper and salt.

Grill or sear tuna over high heat quickly on both sides, until desired doneness is reached. This is best served rare.

Line 4 bowls or plates with lettuce leaves.

Toss beans, potatoes, tomatoes and olives in vinaigrette, adjust seasoning and place on lettuce.

Place cooked tuna on top of salad, arrange egg around salad and garnish with fresh basil.

VEAL FILLING

1 lb (500gr) ground veal
2 tbsp olive oil
1 tsp fennel seed
2 cloves garlic, sliced
1 shallot, sliced
¼ cup whipping cream
¼ cup grated parmesan
1 tbsp chopped oregano
2 tbsp chopped parsley
1 tsp chopped rosemary
salt & pepper

PASTA DOUGH

1 ¼ cups semolina flour
12 egg yolks
1/3 cup cream cheese
1 tsp salt

VEAL RAVIOLI WITH SHEMIJI MUSHROOMS & SAGE BUTTER

Heat olive oil in pan with fennel seed, add garlic and shallot.

Continue cooking without color, add veal and cook until veal is cooked through, season.

Strain veal mixture and then pulse in a food processor. Add rest of ingredients and pulse until all items are mixed together.

Place in refrigerator.

Combine flour and salt in food processor, add cream cheese and mix. Slowly add egg yolks until dough forms balls and is elastic.

Wrap dough in plastic and let rest for 20 minutes.

Using a pasta machine, roll dough out into thin sheets. Place sheet on flat surface and brush half of sheet with egg wash.

Place tablespoon of veal mix every inch along egg washed sheet. Lay other half of pasta on the top and press around veal mix.

Using a crimping wheel cutter, cut out ravioli squares. Sprinkle ravioli with semolina and reserve in fridge until ready to use.

1 cup shemiji mushrooms, or similar

4 tbsp butter

1 clove garlic, thinly sliced

1 shallot, thinly sliced

4 leaves sage

ravioli

salt & pepper

Bring pot of salted water to a boil. Cook ravioli in water for 5 minutes.

While pasta is cooking sauté mushrooms, garlic and shallots in butter until brown.

Lower heat and add whole sage, add pasta and toss until ingredients are well combined, adjust seasoning and serve.

FENNEL APPLE SALAD

1 bulb fennel

1 crisp apple, preferably granny smith

1/4 red pepper

1 tsp chopped chive

2 tsp olive oil

1 tsp white sugar

2 tsp rice wine vinegar

salt & pepper

CITRUS CRÈME FRAÎCHE

1 cup whipping cream

2 tbsp buttermilk

1 tbsp orange juice

1 tsp lemon juice

zest from 1 lemon

salt & sugar to taste

CURED SALMON

1 lb (500gr) fresh salmon fillet, skin on & boneless

½ cup coarse salt

½ cup white sugar

2 tsp fresh dill

1 tsp fresh black pepper

SALMON TRIO

Slice the fennel bulb as thin as possible, combine with julienne (small matchstick cut) apple and red pepper.

In a small jar combine the oil, sugar and cider vinegar, place on lid and shake to dissolve sugar and combine ingredients, season to taste with the salt and pepper.

Toss the finely cut vegetables with the vinaigrette and chives and refrigerate.

Combine whipping cream and buttermilk, cover and rest at room temperature for 12 hours.

Add orange juice, lemon juice and zest, season to taste with the salt and sugar.

For cured salmon, place salmon fillet on a large piece of plastic wrap. Coat with the mixture of salt, sugar, and pepper, use all the salt as any extra will be rinsed off.

It is important to remember to use coarse salt as if you use the fine salt the end product will be way to salty. The large salt crystals will only partly dissolve and the rest will be rinsed off.

Wrap the plastic wrap tightly around fish and place into a baking dish, place a plate on top of the fish to weigh it down slightly, refrigerate.

The next day turn the fish and replace the plate and refrigerate for another 24 hours.

SALMON TARTARE

8 oz (250gr) fresh salmon meat, chopped

1 tbsp chopped capers

1 tbsp chopped red onion

1 tsp chopped basil

1 tbsp lemon juice

1 tbsp virgin olive oil

1 tsp dijon mustard

pinch cayenne

salt & fresh pepper

Rinse off the excess salt and pat dry.

Cover Salmon with freshly chopped dill. At this stage the salmon will keep in the fridge for at least 1 week.

Slice thinly to serve.

Use the same method as above to cure your salmon fillet but use brown sugar instead on white. Use a smoker and smoke salmon until interior temperature reaches 140°F. Cool and use as required.

Combine all the ingredients for the salmon tartare together and adjust seasoning.

Goat Cheese Brûlée

BRÛLÉE
6 egg yolks

1 whole egg

2 cups cereal cream

½ cup goat cheese

salt & pepper to taste

OLIVE CRISPS
9 oz (250 ml) chicken stock
or water

½ cup cornmeal

1 tbsp finely chopped black olives

1 tbsp finely chopped green olives

1 tsp finely chopped fresh
rosemary

salt & fresh ground pepper

GOAT CHEESE BRÛLÉE

This goat cheese appetizer is served warm from under the broiler and is great with fresh French bread, flat bread or the olive crisps that follow.

Preheat oven to 300°F/150°C.

Whisk together egg yolk and egg. Bring cream to a simmer and mix into eggs, add goat cheese and stir until mixture is smooth. Season with salt and pepper and pour into ramekins.

Place ramekins into a baking dish and pour in hot water to reach half way up the sides of the dishes. Cover with foil with a few holes poked into it, and place in oven for 30 minutes.

Check the ramekins, the mixture should be just setting at this point, if still runny bake for further 5 minutes. Remove from baking pan and cool.

To serve drizzle reduced balsamic on top of brûl e and place under broiler until balsamic starts to bubble.

Preheat oven to 350°F/180°C.

Bring stock or water to boil, add the cornmeal in a slow stream stirring constantly, continue to cook until mixture pulls away from the side of the pot. Stir in the olives and rosemary until well blended, season.

Place between two sheets of parchment or wax paper and roll to cracker thickness, cut into desired shapes and bake on a parchment lined or greased cookie sheet for five minutes or until crisp.

1 whole duck

2 oz (56g) lean diced ham

2 oz (56g) skinless pistachios

2 tbsp pink peppercorns

1 tbsp fine chopped rosemary & thyme

2 oz (56g) diced bacon

¼ tsp ground allspice

salt & pepper

2 oz (56ml) brandy

2 oz (56ml) madeira or port wine

5 oz (140gr) lean pork meat

5 oz (140gr) veal

9 oz (250gr) pork belly fat

liver from duck

1 egg

6 oz (170ml) whipping cream

yields 8-10 portions

DUCK, PISTACHIOS & PINK PEPPERCORN TERRINE

Debone duck completely and reserve skin. Remove all meat from legs and breast and keep separated. Cut breast in quarter inch dice and add to ham, pistachios, peppercorns and bacon. Add all spice, seasoning, herbs and alcohol, marinate for at least 2 hours.

Finely blend meat (from duck legs, veal, pork, liver and fat) in food processor, add egg and cream and mix for further 30 seconds. Add to marinated duck breast mixture and fold together.

Test paté by poaching a small amount, adjust seasoning accordingly.

Line terrine or bread tin with duck skin and fill with paté mix, cover with remaining skin.

Place weight on top of paté, put terrine into baking tray half filled with warm water and cook in moderately hot oven 350°F/ 180°C for approximately 1 hour.

Terrine can be tested by inserting a long needle or fine knife blade into centre of pate. If needle is hot when withdrawn meat is cooked or cook until interior temperature is 140°C.

Remove from water and cool for at least 24 hours before serving. Slice as required.

Serve with mustard melons and cranberry relish.

VANILLA CURED WILD SALMON

1 side fresh salmon, boneless with skin on

½ cup coarse salt

¼ cup sugar

¼ cup golden sugar

1 orange, sliced

1 lemon, sliced

3 tbsp vanilla tea leaves

10 pieces star anise

1 tsp cloves

Combine salt and sugars together and cover salmon flesh evenly with mixture, skin side down. Sprinkle fish with tea leaves and cover with rest of ingredients.

Lay tray on salmon and press down with light weights. Refrigerate for 36-48 hours until salmon is cured and firm to touch.

Remove curing ingredients from fish. Serve thin slices over fennel slaw or tossed greens.

MUSHROOM PÂTÉ

2 cups button mushrooms

2 cups portabella mushrooms

2 tbsp butter

2 tbsp canola oil

4 cloves garlic

2 shallots

2 cups cream cheese

1 cup mascarpone cheese

½ cup bread crumbs

salt & pepper

Clean mushrooms.

Heat butter and oil in saucepan, sauté mushrooms, garlic and shallots over medium heat for approximately 20 minutes until moisture has evaporated.

Transfer to a food processor and pulse leaving mixture slightly chunky.

Cool to room temperature and fold in the 2 cheeses, add bread crumbs and adjust seasoning. Place mixture into buttered ramekins and bake in preheated oven at 372°F/190°C for 5 minutes.

Serve with crusty sliced baguette.

QUINCE COMPOTE

1 cup quince, peeled and seeded, quarter inch dice

½ cup butternut squash, quarter inch dice

½ cup red onion, diced

¼ cup dried apricots, diced

2 tbsp sugar

¼ cup raspberry vinegar

¼ cup apple juice

2 tbsp red currant jelly

1 star anise

½ tsp fresh ground black pepper

4 legs duck confit, remove from fat

2 tbsp aged balsamic

1 cup baby lettuce

DUCK LEG CONFIT WITH QUINCE COMPOTE

For the quince compote, combine all of ingredients together in a saucepan and simmer over a medium heat. Continue cooking until half of liquid have evaporated, adjust seasoning. Let cool to room temperature.

Place duck legs on baking sheet and place in preheated oven 400°F/200°C for approximately 8-10 minutes or until skin is crisp. Remove from pan and place on napkin to remove any excess fat.

To serve place duck on compote and garnish with baby lettuce and drizzle of balsamic.

4 duck legs
1 tbsp coarse salt
1 tbsp fresh ground pepper
4 cloves garlic
4 sprigs fresh thyme
2 sprigs fresh rosemary
2 bay leaves
4 lb (1.8 kg) duck or pork fat

DUCK CONFIT

In a shallow glass or ceramic dish place duck legs, sprinkle both sides with salt and pepper. Note that you need to use coarse or kosher salt or the finished duck legs will be too salty. Place thyme, bay leaves, rosemary and garlic evenly over the meat, cover and refrigerate overnight.

If using the duck or pork fat place in a heavy bottomed saucepot and slowly heat too render out the fat; cook until all that remains is clear liquid and crisp rendered solids.

Strain through a fine sieve or cheesecloth and discard the solids. Refrigerate until ready to use.

Reheat fat in a large pot until bubbling.

Remove duck legs from cure and pat dry.

Add duck legs to rendered fat and bring to a simmer. Cook uncovered for 1 to 1 ½ hours or until meat is tender and falling off the bone and lightly brown.

Remove from the heat, remove the meat and place in a glass or ceramic dish and strain the fat over top of the meat to cover completely. Cool and refrigerate until needed. Reheat the duck before using to drain off extra fat.

If the meat is completely covered with fat it will keep in the refrigerator for up to 1 month.

1 tbsp olive oil
¼ cup minced shallots
1 cup fine chopped mushrooms
¼ cup fine chopped carrot
¼ cup fine chopped leek
¼ cup fine chopped celery
2 tsp minced garlic
½ cup white burgundy wine
1 cup whipping cream
1 cup chopped parsley
1 can (24) escargot
½ cup chicken stock
salt & fresh ground black pepper

ESCARGOT BOURGUIGNON

Heat oil in sauté pan.

Sweat shallots, leeks, celery, carrot and garlic without color. Add mushrooms and lightly brown.

Add wine and reduce until liquid has evaporated.

Add rest of ingredients and reduce by half, adjust seasoning and serve with crusty baguette.

8 oz (225gr) dried salt cod
1 lb (450gr) picked cooked crab meat
flaked cod
1 lime, juice only
2 tbsp chopped cilantro
1 tsp chopped dill
1 jalepeno fine chopped
¼ red onion fine diced
1 tbsp worcestershire sauce
2 eggs
½ cup bread crumbs
salt & pepper to season

SALT COD & CRAB CAKES

Soak cod in cold water for at least 24 hours, during this time change water at least twice.

Skin cod and poach in simmering milk for approximately 5 minutes. Cool fish and dry. Flake meat removing any bones and skin.

Combine all ingredients together adding bread crumbs as required to bind ingredients. Scoop cakes out with a 2 oz. ladle onto floured surface. Slightly flatten into cake shape.

Fry over medium heat in butter until golden brown.

TERRINE

1 lobe foie gras, approx. 1 lb (450gr)

½ cup cognac

sea salt & fresh ground white pepper

RELISH

¼ cup sundried cranberries

¼ cup sundried cherries

¼ cup dried apricots, cut into small dice

¼ cup dried blueberries

3 tbsp red onion, fine diced

¼ cup sugar

¼ cup raspberry vinegar

2 tbsp red currant jelly

½ cup water

salt & fresh ground pepper

FOIE GRAS TERRINE WITH BERRY RELISH

Take foie gras from refrigerator and place on cutting board for 30 minutes at room temperature.

Using a small sharp knife split open liver being careful not to cut right through liver and skin. Using the point of your knife start removing veins pushing the liver open as you progress. When veins have been removed season with cognac, salt and pepper.

Line and overlap a suitable sized terrine with plastic film. Press foie gras into terrine until level with top. Cover foie gras with plastic film overlap.

Place terrine in a deep tray with warm water reaching half way up terrine. Place in preheated oven 250°F/130°C and cook for 15 minutes. Remove from water and refrigerate at least overnight.

For the relish, combine all ingredients together and simmer over medium heat until almost all liquid has evaporated.

To unmould foie gras, place terrine in warm water for a few seconds, then carefully unwrap foie gras from plastic wrap and place on cutting board.

Warm a thin knife in water and cut one slice approximately a ¼ inch thick. Place 1 tbsp of berry relish on one side of plate and lean foie gras against relish.

Pan Seared Quail

RISOTTO

1 cup cooked barley

1 tsp chopped shallot

1 tbsp butter

1 tsp chopped fresh thyme

½ cup chicken stock

1 tbsp grated parmesan

¼ cup white wine

¼ cup cream

salt and pepper

4 x boneless quail

BLUEBERRY GLAZE

1 cup fresh or frozen blueberries

1 cup game or meat glaze

½ cup port

1 tbsp butter

1 tsp oil

1 tsp finely chopped shallot

salt & pepper

2 tbsp reduced aged balsamic

PAN SEARED QUAIL ON BARLEY RISOTTO, BLUEBERRY GLAZE

To make risotto, heat butter in non stick pan, add shallots and continue cooking without color. Add rest of ingredients except cheese and simmer until risotto starts to thicken. Add cheese and adjust seasoning, Keep warm, add hot stock if risotto thickens before you are ready to serve.

Heat frying pan over high heat. Season quail and brown in butter and oil on all sides, this should take only 2-3 minutes.

Remove quail when desired doneness is reached and let rest.

Add chopped shallot to pan and brown, add port and cook until evaporated.

Add glaze and reduce by half, pass sauce through fine sieve, add blueberries and bring to a simmer, adjust seasoning.

To assemble, place risotto in center of plate or bowl with quail arranged on top. Drizzle sauce around risotto and spoon streaks of balsamic with sauce.

Pheasant Spring Rolls

SPRING ROLLS

1 pheasant, may substitute with chicken or duck

1 carrot, peeled

1 zucchini

1 red Pepper,

1 yellow pepper

1 cup bean sprouts

2 leaves bok choy

1 cup snow peas

1 tbsp ginger, finely chopped

½ cup fresh cilantro, chopped

½ cup soya sauce

3 tbsp sesame oil

1 tsp hot chili sauce

PLUM QUINCE COMPOTE

2 quince, peeled, cored & diced

3 plums, sliced

1 tbsp ginger, finely chopped

1 red onion, finely diced

2 tbsp brown sugar

½ cup rice wine vinegar

3 pieces star anise

salt & pepper

PHEASANT SPRING ROLLS WITH PLUM QUINCE COMPOTE

Season and roast pheasant at 375°F/190°C until fully cooked but not dry, approximately 1 hour, remove from pan and cool.

Cut all vegetables into julienne (finely cut sticks). Remove meat from pheasant carcass and cut into julienne.

Heat a wok or sauté pan over high heat, add oil, ginger and vegetables and sauté without color until vegetables start to go limp and still slightly crisp. Add soya, chili and pheasant, continue cooking for further minute. Mixture may now be slightly thickened with a little corn starch and water mixture if desired. Remove from pan and add cilantro, adjust seasoning and cool.

Place the spring roll wrap on a dry table with one corner pointing to top of table. Lightly dampen the top 2 sides with water. Place approximately 2 heaped tablespoons of mix in center of wrapper. First fold the bottom corner of wrapper over mixture, then fold corners in and roll towards top until mixture is surrounded with wrapper.

To serve preheat oil and fry as required.

For plum quince compote, place all ingredients in saucepan and simmer until liquid has evaporated. Remove star anise and serve at room temperature.

Braised Short Rib & Bacon Wrapped Dates

SHORT RIBS

4 x meaty short ribs

4 cups veal stock

1 cup red wine

2 cups diced onion, celery & carrot

2 cloves garlic

1 cup fresh thyme, rosemary and bay leaf

3 tbsp olive oil

salt & pepper

DATES

12 slices double smoked bacon, thinly sliced

12 pieces fresh dated, pitted

BRAISED SHORT RIB & BACON WRAPPED DATES

Season ribs with salt and pepper, then sear in pan with oil until browned.

Remove meat and add vegetables to pan and continue cooking until brown, add wine and reduce.

Add garlic, veal stock and ribs back into the pan. Bring to a boil, cover and place in preheated oven 350°F/180°C for 1 hour.

Continue baking ribs for a further hour but baste ribs every 20 minutes.

Finally remove cover and cook for a further 15 minutes at 400°F/200°C.

Remove meat from sauce, strain sauce and reduce until sauce thickens, adjust seasoning.

Wrap each date with a slice of bacon.

Fry over medium heat until crisp.

To serve, arrange dates around heated spare rib and drizzle with sauce.

Garnish with Mache lettuce or arugula.

POLENTA FILLING

½ cup corn meal

1 cup milk

2 tbsp butter

1 clove garlic

1 tsp chopped truffles

salt & pepper

CELERIAC SHEETS

2 pieces celeriac (celery root) peeled

3 cups milk

pinch nutmeg & salt

2 x fresh lobsters

BUTTER POACHED LOBSTER WITH REVERSED RAVIOLI

Bring milk and garlic to a boil. Remove garlic and reduce to a simmer. Slowly add cornmeal stirring continuously until it is thick. Add chopped truffles and adjust seasoning.

Thinly slice celeriac into circles.

Bring milk and seasoning to a simmer and poach celeriac for about 10 minutes until soft. Drain and cool.

Lay out 12 sheets of blanched celeriac using only unbroken pieces. Place a tablespoon of polenta in center of each slice then place another slice on top. Press down around edges and cut out into a circle, refrigerate.

Bring large pot of salted water to a boil. Remove tails from lobster and reserve. Separate claws from knuckles and boil for 7 minutes.

Remove from pot and cool in iced water.

With a knife and kitchen shears remove cooked meat from claws and knuckles. With the tail, crack shell and carefully remove meat.

To finish dish melt half pound of butter over medium heat until it is bubbling. Add lobster tail and season with salt and pepper, cook for 7-8 minutes.

While tail is cooking sauté ravioli and claw meat in some good olive oil, lightly browning ravioli on both sides.

Arrange lobster on top of ravioli, drizzle with remaining oil.

For added texture and sweetness incorporate a large seared scallop with this dish.

PATE

14 oz (400gr) chicken liver

6 shallots, chopped

1 clove garlic, chopped

1 tsp oil

1 sprig fresh thyme, leaves only chopped

½ cup cognac

½ cup madeira wine

½ cup port

14 oz (400gr) butter

5 eggs

salt & pepper

RELISH

1 cup dried figs

½ cup dried sour cherries

½ cup fresh or frozen cherries

1 large orange, zest and juice

½ cup port

¼ tsp dry mustard

pinch cayenne

¼ tsp cinnamon

¼ tsp salt

½ cup sugar

CHICKEN LIVER PÂTÉ WITH SOUR CHERRY RELISH

Sweat shallots, thyme and garlic over medium heat with oil, add liquor and reduce by 2/3, then cool.

Place remaining liquid, shallots and garlic in a food processor with chicken livers and puree together.

Slowly add the melted butter and eggs one at a time until mixture is well combined and has a smooth texture, season.

Pass mixture through a fine sieve then pour into a terrine mold lined with plastic wrap.

Bake at 300°F/150°C for 25 minutes in a shallow pan with enough warm water to come half way up the terrine mold.

Mixture can also be divided into smaller individual cocottes, cooking time will be shorter.

Cool overnight, slice and serve with relish and crusty bread.

For the relish, dice all the fruits, combine with rest of ingredients in saucepan and simmer over medium heat until nearly all of the liquid has evaporated.

VENISON PÂTÉ

1 lb (450gr) venison meat diced into cubes

12 oz (340gr) pork belly fat diced into cubes

7 oz (200gr) duck or chicken liver

1 shallot, chopped

2 tbsp pistachios

2 tbsp oil

1 tbsp chopped fresh thyme

½ tsp juniper berries, crushed

¼ cup brandy or cognac

¼ tsp allspice, ground

salt & fresh ground black pepper

1 egg

¼ cup whipping cream

12 slices pancetta

Heat oil in frying pan, add shallot and sauté without colour, add liver, thyme, juniper, allspice and brandy. Sauté briefly until liver changes color.

Transfer to a bowl and cool. Add venison, pork, seasoning and mix well. Cover and refrigerate for one hour.

In a food processor chop pâté mix in small batches until well blended and meat is in small pieces.

Add egg, cream and pistachios and mix well, adjust seasoning.

Line a terrine mold or bread tin with cling film, then line with pancetta. Fill the mold with pâté mix and cover with pancetta, cover with foil. Place mold in deep tray and add water up to 2/3 of terrine mold.

Poach in oven 370°F/190°C for approximately 50 minutes or until center of pâté is warm.

When cool remove from mould and cling film, place on cutting board.

To serve slice pate ¼ inch thick and serve with relish and fresh bread.

4 x meaty short ribs

1 onion diced

1 carrot diced

1 stalk celery diced

2 tomatoes, chopped

2 tbsp tomato paste

2 bay leaves

4 sprig of fresh thyme

1 cup red wine

4 cups beef or game stock

salt & pepper to season

RISOTTO

1 cup arborio rice

1 cup morel mushrooms, or other seasonal mushroom, cleaned

2 tbsp butter

1 shallot, finely chopped

½ cup white wine

5 cups vegetable or chicken stock

¼ cup grated parmesan

½ tsp truffle oil, (optional)

BRAISED SHORT RIBS ON MOREL MUSHROOM RISOTTO

Trim excess fat from spare ribs and season with salt and pepper.

Heat heavy pan over medium heat sear ribs until brown on all sides, add vegetables and continue browning.

Add tomato and paste, continue cooking over heat for a further few minutes. Add wine, stock, thyme and bay leaf.

Place lid on pan and put into preheated oven 300°F/150°C until meat starts to fall off of bone approximately 2 hours.

Add stock or water as required, meat should always be covered with liquid. Remove meat from sauce and let cool.

Strain sauce and reduce until sauce starts to thicken, adjust seasoning.

Melt butter in heavy saucepan; add shallot and sauté without color. Add rice and continue cooking until for further minute.

Add wine and stir until it has evaporated, add stock one cup at a time stirring frequently.

After 3 cups of stock have been absorbed by the rice, add mushrooms. and remaining stock, cook until rice is still slightly crunchy in the center.

Add parmesan and more liquid if required. Adjust seasoning.

To serve place risotto in center of large bowl, remove meat from bone and slice.

Arrange around risotto and drizzle sauce.

Garnish with shaved parmesan.

Mountain Minestrone

SOUPS

Lobster & Squash Chowder

ARUGULA PESTO

1 cup fresh arugula leaves

1 tbsp tarragon leaves

½ cup fresh grated parmesan

½ cup olive oil

fresh ground pepper

LOBSTER BISQUE

2 small lobsters

½ cup butter

2 carrots, diced

1 leek, diced

1 onion, diced

3 stalks celery, diced

12 peppercorns

4 bayleaf

1 tsp fresh thyme

5 cups cream

½ cup brandy

1 cup white wine

4 cups fish stock

salt, pepper & cayenne to season

SOUP

2 tbsp butter

1 cup leek, ¼ inch dice

4 cups assorted squash, ¼ inch dice (blanched)

16 red and orange cherry tomatoes (halved)

lobster meat in large dice

LOBSTER & SQUASH CHOWDER WITH ARUGULA PESTO

Combine all ingredients for the argula pesto together and purée Boil large pot of water seasoned with diced carrot, onion, celery, peppercorns, bay leaf and salt.

Cook 2 lobsters in rolling boiling water for 4 minutes. Discard water and refresh lobsters under cold iced water. Carefully remove meat from shells and refrigerate, save shells.

Melt butter over medium heat in heavy saucepan, add lobster shells and sauté in butter until they start to color.

Add coarse diced vegetables and continue cooking until limp, add wine, brandy and stocks.

Bring to simmer and add cream, seasoning and herbs. Simmer for approximately one hour. Consistency should be like cream, add water as required.

Strain through fine sieve and adjust seasoning.

To assemble chowder, sauté leek without color in butter, add squash, lobster and lobster cream. Bring to simmer for 1 minute, adjust seasoning and ladle into warm soup bowls.

Drizzle with arugula pesto and serve.

STOCK

4½ lb (2kg) game bones
1 chopped carrot
1 chopped onion
1 chopped leek
3 stalks chopped celery
2 bay leaves
10 crushed juniper berries
10 crushed peppercorns
fresh thyme

CLARIFICATION

1 lb (450 gr) ground game meat
1 carrot
1 onion
1 stalk celery
3 egg whites
1 tbsp tomato paste
1 cup water

GAME CONSOMMÉ

Lightly roast bones until golden brown. Put all ingredients for stock into a pot and add enough cold water to cover bones. Bring to a boil then simmer for 3 hours, add water as it evaporates so that bones are always covered. Strain stock, cool and refrigerate.

For the clarification, pass vegetables through course grinder or finely dice. Combine with rest of ingredients and mix well together.

Stir mixture into cold stock in heavy sauce pan. Slowly bring to simmer over medium heat.

While bringing to a simmer carefully scrape bottom of sauce pan to make sure raft is not sticking. Do not stir stock or boil as this will cloud your consommé.

Simmer for approximately 45 minutes, meat should rise to surface and act as a filter.

Turn heat off and let rest for 15 minutes.

With a ladle carefully strain consommé through a fine sieve, cheese cloth or coffee filter.

Adjust seasoning as required.

SOUP

4 cups butternut squash, peeled, seeded, large dice

1 cup apple juice

2 cups diced sweet potato

1 onion diced

¼ cup butter

1 tsp chopped ginger

1 tsp allspice

1 tsp cinnamon

½ tsp nutmeg

6 cups chicken or vegetable stock

1 cup cream

salt & fresh ground pepper

PESTO

½ cup toasted pumpkin seeds

1 tbsp fresh thyme

1 tbsp fresh parsley

¼ cup hempseed or canola oil

¼ cup grated parmesan

blend all ingredients together

CHOWDER

I cup butternut squash in ¼ inch dice

1 cup sweet corn kernels

½ cup sweet potato, ¼ inch dice

2 tbsp butter

salt & fresh ground pepper

ROASTED SQUASH & CORN CHOWDER WITH PUMPKIN SEED THYME PESTO

Season squash with all spice, cinnamon, nutmeg and salt and pepper.

Place on baking sheet with apple juice and bake in preheated oven 350°F/180°C for 30 minutes, cover squash with foil when light brown . .

Sauté onion and ginger in butter in saucepan without color. Add roasted squash and rest of ingredients and simmer for approximately 30 minutes or until sweet potatoes are soft.

Purée in food processor then pass through medium sieve.

Keep warm.

Melt butter in sauce pan, add squash, corn and sweet potato, sauté without color.

Add roasted squash purée and bring to simmer for 10 minutes, adjust seasoning.

To serve ladle chowder into warm bowl and drizzle with pesto.

BUFFALO, VEGETABLE & BARLEY BROTH

4 cups game or beef stock

4 cups water

1 cup buffalo meat, finely diced

2 tbsp canola oil

1 onion, diced

½ cup carrot, diced

½ cup leek, diced

½ cup celery, diced

½ cup barley, cooked

1 tbsp fresh thyme, chopped

salt & fresh ground pepper

Heat oil in sauce pan, add meat and sauté until meat is brown.

Add vegetables and continue cooking until vegetables are limp but not brown.

Add rest of ingredients and bring to a simmer.

Reduce liquid by half, add thyme and adjust seasoning.

MUSHROOM & CELERIAC SOUP

2 tbsp butter

1 tsp chopped thyme

1 onion, diced

1 clove garlic, crushed

2 cups celery root

1 lb (450gr) button mushrooms

1 cup dried wild mushroom, soaked in warn water

3 cups cream

3 cups half and half cream

6 cups chicken or vegetable stock

salt & fresh ground pepper

Melt butter in saucepan, add onions, garlic and button mushrooms and sauté until all moisture has evaporated.

Add rest of ingredients and bring to simmer, reduce by half.

Purée in food processor, adjust seasoning and serve.

LEEK & POTATO SOUP

2 tbsp butter

1 onion ¼ inch dice

1 large leek ¼ inch dice

2 potatoes, peeled cut in ¼ inch dice

4 cups vegetable or chicken stock

1 cup cream

1 tsp chopped fresh thyme

salt, fresh ground pepper, ground nutmeg

Melt butter in saucepan over medium heat, add onion and leek and cook until transparent without color.

Add rest of ingredients and simmer for 30 minutes, stirring occasionally.

Adjust seasoning and serve.

This soup may also be puréed if you prefer a smooth texture.

MOUNTAIN MINESTRONE

3 tbsp olive oil

1 clove garlic crushed

1 red onion ½ inch dice

2 oz (60gr) diced pancetta

1 green zucchini, ½ inch dice

1 yellow zucchini, ½ inch dice

1 cup cabbage, ¼ inch dice

1 leek ½ inch dice

1 cup cherry tomatoes cut in half

½ cup cooked navy beans

2 cups tomato juice

3 cups vegetable stock

1 tbsp chopped basil

½ cup orzo pasta

salt & fresh ground pepper

grated parmesan

Heat olive oil in saucepan, add onion, garlic, pancetta, zucchini, leek and cabbage.

Sauté vegetables without color then add tomato juice, stock, beans and seasoning, simmer for 25 minutes.

Add cherry tomatoes, orzo and basil, simmer for a further 10 minutes, adjust seasoning and serve topped with grated parmesan.

see photo on page 36

1 cup yellow onion, diced

2 poblano peppers, roasted, peeled and seeded

1 large potato, peeled, cut into small cubes

1 tsp salt

1 tsp black pepper

1 tsp fresh thyme

1 cup fresh spinach

10 cups vegetable stock or chicken stock

ROASTED POBLANO PEPPER SOUP

Roast, peel and seed poblano peppers. Add all ingredients to a large pot and bring to boil. Adjust heat to simmer and continue cooking for 30 minutes.

Purée to a smooth consistency and adjust seasoning. To finish soup add half cup whipping cream, and garnish soup with crumbled goat cheese and chopped cilantro.

1lb (450gr) vine ripe whole tomatoes, core removed, diced

1 green pepper, seeded, diced

1 hard boiled egg

1 medium red onion, diced

1 cup long english cucumber (seeds removed)

1 tbsp garlic

1 cup tomato juice

½ cup ketchup

1 cup mayonnaise

¼ cup olive oil

¼ cup red wine vinegar

1 tbsp white sugar

¼ cup basil leaves

1 tsp ground sweet paprika

1 tbsp ground almonds

salt & white pepper to taste

CHILLED GAZPACHO SOUP

In a food processor combine green pepper, eggs, onion, cucumber, garlic, tomato juice, olive oil and vinegar.

Add rest of ingredients and blend together. Adjust seasoning.

Refrigerate this mixture for at least 12 hours.

Remove soup from refrigerator an hour before serving and re adjust seasoning.

Serve in chilled bowl and garnish with chopped chives.

3 tbsp olive oil

1 tbsp butter

3 cups onion, assorted types, finely sliced

2 cloves garlic, finely chopped

8 cups beef stock

1 cup white wine

1 tbsp fresh thyme, chopped

2 bay leaves

2 cup white cheese, grated

8 slices baguette ¼ inch slice, dried

salt & fresh ground black pepper

BAKED ONION SOUP

Heat oil and butter in saucepan, add onion and sweat over medium heat.

Continue cooking until onions are well browned and starting to caramelize.

Add garlic and sauté for further 2 minutes, add wine and incorporate well into onions. Add bay leaf, thyme and beef stock, bring to simmer and cover pot, then cook for approximately 30 minutes or until soup has reduced by half. Taste soup and adjust seasoning.

Ladle soup into four bowls, place baguette slices on top and sprinkle cheese over bread.

Place bowls under preheated broiler and cook until cheese is melted and starts to brown.

Heirloom Beet Soup

HEIRLOOM BEET SOUP

½ cup onions, diced

¼ cup celery, diced

1 cup red beets, diced

¼ cup fennel, diced

¼ cup carrots, diced

½ cup cabbage, diced

½ cup yellow beets, diced

3 tbsp vegetable oil

6 cups vegetable stock

salt & pepper to taste

1 tbsp lemon juice

3 tbsp fresh dill, chopped

4 tbsp sour cream

Heat oil in a saucepot and sauté vegetable until transparent.

Add stock and bring to a boil and reduce to a simmer and continue to cook until the vegetables are tender.

Season with salt, pepper and add juice of the lemon.

To serve mix in fresh dill and top with the sour cream.

SALMON CHOWDER

2 tbsp butter

1 onion in ¼ inch dice

1 leek ¼ inch dice

1 small fennel bulb ¼ inch dice

1 large red potato, skin on ¼ inch dice

1 cup corn kernels

8 oz (225gr) boneless skinless salmon cubes, ½ inch dice

4 cups fish or vegetable stock

1 cup cream

2 tbsp chopped parsley

pinch cayenne

salt & pepper

Melt butter over medium heal in saucepan, add onion, leek and fennel continue cooking without color until vegetables are limp.

Add stock, cream, corn and potatoes and simmer for 20 minutes.

Add salmon, parsley and seasoning and simmer for a further 5 minutes, adjust seasoning and serve.

Endive and Radicchio Salad

SALADS

ARTICHOKE PESTO SALAD

1 cup artichoke hearts, cooked & cut into quarters

1 cup small button mushroom caps, cleaned

½ cup cherry tomatoes

½ cup pitted black olives

4 tbsp basil pesto

¼ cup grated parmesan

1 cup baby arugula leaves

fresh ground black pepper

Combine artichokes, mushrooms, olives and cherry tomatoes with pesto, add fresh ground pepper and toss together.

This can be served immediately or left to marinate for 30 minutes.

When ready to serve fold arugula into artichoke salad and place in serving bowls, sprinkle cheese over top of salad, serve immediately.

MISO VINAIGRETTE

¼ cup miso paste

½ cup rice wine vinegar

2 tsp wasabi powder

4 tsp soya sauce

2 tsp sugar

½ tsp garlic

½ tsp asian fish sauce

1 1/3 cups canola oil

2 tbsp green onions, chopped

4 tsp toasted sesame seeds

This is one of the most requested recipes from our kitchen at Emerald Lake Lodge, it makes a regular appearance on our summer menu and is great with fresh summer vegetables.

Again for this recipe we use the yellow or red miso paste when preparing the vinaigrette.

In a large bowl combine the miso paste and wasabi, add the vinegar and stir to dissolve the paste and wasabi.

Add the soya sauce, sugar, garlic and ginger and whisk to combine. Add oil, green onions and sesame seeds.

DRESSING

½ red onions, finely diced

½ cup white vinegar

¼ cup olive oil

½ cup canola oil

1 tbsp fresh chives, chopped

1 tsp sugar

salt & pepper

SALAD

1 head radicchio

2 heads belgium endive

1 apple

1 pear

4 oz (115gr) gorgonzola cheese, or other soft blue cheese

2 oz (60g) roasted walnuts

2 egg yolks

1 tbsp dried mustard

1 lemon, juiced

1 clove garlic, minced

1 tbsp minced anchovy

1 tbsp worcestershire sauce

2 cups canola oil

½ cup white wine vinegar

fresh ground black pepper

3 tbsp fresh grated parmesan, optional or sprinkle on salad

salt to taste

ENDIVE & RADICCHIO SALAD

For the dressing, combine all ingredients together and adjust seasoning. Best made a day in advance so flavours can mellow and onions soften.

To build the salad, tear the radicchio into bite sized pieces and trim endive placing both into a bowl. Thinly slice the apple and pear and toss with radicchio and endive.

Toss salad with enough dressing to lightly coat, divide evenly on four plates or bowls. Top with crumbled Gorgonzola and walnuts.

see photo on page 48

CAESAR DRESSING

In a food processor combine egg yolks, mustard, lemon juice, garlic and worcestershire sauce until well mixed.

Slowly drizzle oil onto egg mix, when dressing thickens alternate oil with vinegar until both are incorporated into dressing.

Season with black pepper and salt if required.

FENNEL SLAW

2 bulbs fennel
1 red onion
1 yellow pepper
1 cup cucumber, cut into fine slices
1 tbsp mint, chopped
1 tbls basil, chopped
½ cup canola oil
½ cup rice wine vinegar
1 tbls sugar
1 tsp salt
 fresh ground pepper

Trim fennel and separate layers from bulb and cut into fine strips.

Slice onion and pepper into fine strips and mix with fennel and cucumber.

Combine rest of ingredients together adjust seasoning and pour over fennel mix.

Marinate for up to 45 minutes then drain dressing from slaw. This can be used for salad dressing later.

This slaw pares well with any fish dish or as a side salad.

COUSCOUS SALAD

1 cup couscous
½ cup cucumber, finely diced
½ cup vine tomatoes, diced
¼ cup red onion, finely diced
½ cup virgin olive oil
2 lemons, juice only
1 lime, juice only
¼ cup fresh basil, chopped
¼ cup mint, chopped
¼ cup warm water
1 tsp kosher salt
fresh ground pepper

Combine all ingredients together and cover with plastic wrap, allow to rest for 2 hours,

Stir a few times to incorporate flavors.

Adjust seasoning and refrigerate for up to 2 days

4 quail

MARINADE
½ cup red wine
2 tbsp olive oil
1 tbsp chopped fresh thyme
1 orange, zest and juice
1 tbsp crushed juniper

VINAIGRETTE
½ cup grape seed or olive oil
3 tbsp raspberry vinegar
3 tbsp saskatoon puree, or other berry puree
1 tsp liquid honey
salt & fresh ground pepper

4 portions mixed baby lettuce
¼ cup saskatoon berries

GRILLED QUAIL, BABY GREENS & SASKATOON BERRY VINAIGRETTE

Split quail down backbone and remove rib and wing bones. Marinate bird for up to 2 hours.

Combine all ingredients for the vinaigrette together and adjust seasoning.

Remove quail from marinade and pat dry on towel.

Grill birds on preheated grill for approximately 3 minutes on each side.

Combine lettuce and berries with 2/3 of vinaigrette and place in center of plate or bowl.

Place quail on salad and drizzle remaining vinaigrette around salad.

Grilled Asparagus & Goat Cheese

½ cup balsamic vinegar

1½ lb (680gr) Asparagus

2 tbsp olive oil

½ tsp kosher salt

¼ cup virgin olive oil

2 tbsp fresh basil, chopped

2 tbsp red pepper, finely diced

¼ cup goat cheese

½ tsp sugar

salt & fresh ground pepper

GRILLED ASPARAGUS & GOAT CHEESE

Reduce balsamic in saucepan over medium heat until it starts to thicken. Do not over reduce as balsamic will thicken while cooling. Set aside.

Trim asparagus to the point where they start to get woody, usually ¾ of the way down from the spears. If asparagus are the thin green variety they will not need to be peeled, if they are the larger green variety or white asparagus they will need to be peeled, starting just below the spears.

Preheat broiler, roll asparagus in oil and season with salt.

Place asparagus on broiler and grill, rolling asparagus every 30 seconds until they are evenly cooked with light brown grill marks. Asparagus should still have a crisp snap to them and not be limp.

Place asparagus on a clean cloth to remove any dark oil, then divide on plates.

Combine oil, basil, red pepper, sugar and seasoning together, adjust seasoning.

To assemble, spoon dressing on asparagus just below tips. Sprinkle goat cheese over asparagus then drizzle half a teaspoon of balsamic over plate.

4 boneless squab breasts
4 portions mixed baby greens

VINAIGRETTE
¼ cup canola oil
¼ cup walnut oil
¼ cup fig balsamic vinegar
1 tsp sugar
salt & pepper

CHEESE CUPS
1 cup grated white cheddar cheese
fresh ground pepper

FIG PATE
2 Figs in small dice
¼ cup roasted chopped walnuts
2 tbls. Fig balsamic vinegar
½ tsp chopped fresh thyme
seasoning

SQUAB BREAST WITH FIG WALNUT OIL VINAIGRETTE

For the vinaigrette, combine oils and vinegar together and adjust seasoning.

Warm a nonstick frying pan over medium heat. Sprinkle thin layer of cheese in a four inch circle, grate fresh pepper over cheese.

Melt cheese and cook until it starts to brown slightly. Carefully remove cheese pancake and drape over back of a cup to form a basket. Let cool.

Combine all ingredients for the fig pâté together and put to one side.

Season Squab breasts with salt and generous amounts of fresh pepper.

Heat a frying pan with a little oil and sear breasts with skin side down first. Place in 375°F/190°C oven for 5-6 minutes. Remove breasts from pan and let rest for 5 minutes before slicing.

To assemble salad, toss lettuce with enough vinaigrette to lightly coat and place in cheddar cups at top of plate. Pour rest of vinaigrette around plate.

Place fig and walnut mixture on the plate and slice squab breast thinly.

WALNUT VINAIGRETTE

3 tbsp grainy mustard

1 tbsp dijon mustard

1 shallot, finely diced

1 egg yolk

¼ cup white wine vinegar

¾ cup olive oil

½ cup walnut oil

1 tbsp sugar

salt & fresh ground pepper

SALAD

2 heads baby frisée lettuce, can be substituted with other robust salad

½ cup bacon lardons (thick bacon strips cooked crisp)

½ cup cherry tomatoes

¼ cup herb croutons

4 fresh eggs

LYONNAISE STYLE FRISÉE SALAD WITH WALNUT VINAIGRETTE

Whisk together shallots, egg yolk, mustards and vinegar. Slowly add oils until blended, add seasoning. This will make about 3 cups of dressing but will keep for several weeks refrigerated.

Add 2 tablespoons of vinegar and a pinch of salt to 4 cups simmering water.

Crack eggs into water and poach to desired doneness.

Toss lettuce, bacon, tomatoes and croutons with enough dressing to lightly coat, season with fresh ground pepper.

Place salad in center of plate and top with warm poached egg and serve.

Summer Tomatoes With
Olive Crostini

OLIVE TAPENADE

1 cup pitted green and black olives, finely chopped

2 tbsp chopped parsley

1 tbsp chopped basil

1 tsp dijon mustard

1 tbsp olive oil

½ tsp minced garlic, (optional)

fresh ground black pepper to taste

4 x ¼ inch slices baguette

6-8 ripe tomatoes

1 head belgium endive

1 cup arugula salad

aged balsamic

virgin olive oil

soft goat cheese

2 cups rice wine vinegar

3 tbsp dried lavender

2/3 cup honey

2 tbsp dijon mustard

1 lemon, zest and juice

salt & pepper

SUMMER TOMATOES WITH OLIVE CROSTINI

Combine all ingredients for the olive tapenade together and let rest for at least 30 minutes before using.

Drizzle baguette slices with olive oil and bake until light brown in oven.

To serve cover toasts with olive mix and place on plate.

Slice tomatoes, clean endive and lettuce and arrange both on plate. Drizzle with olive oil and aged balsamic.

Spoon goat cheese on olive crostini and serve.

Garnish with sea salt and course ground pepper.

LAVENDER FIREWEED HONEY VINAIGRETTE

Combine the rice wine vinegar with the dried lavender, bring to boil and reduce by half. Strain and cool.

Add remaining ingredients to vinegar reduction and whisk together. Slowly add 1 cup olive oil, adjust seasoning and use as required.

Vanilla Butter
Poached Ahi Tuna

FISH

Mussels Provençal

MUSSELS PROVENÇAL

2 lbs (900gr) fresh mussels

4 tbsp olive oil

3 roma tomatoes diced

4 cloves garlic sliced

4 tbsp capers chopped

2 shallots sliced

pinch crushed chili

½ cup white wine

¼ cup fish stock

½ cup chopped parsley

3 tbsp unsalted butter

salt & fresh ground pepper

Rinse and de-beard mussels.

Heat oil in sauté pan, add garlic and shallots brown slightly then add tomatoes, capers, and chilies.

Add mussels, wine, and stock. Cover until mussels have all opened about 5 minutes.

Remove lid and add butter to the broth to thicken. Toss in parsley and season to taste.

Serve with crisp French fries and lemon mayonnaise or crusty baguette.

4 salmon fillets

2 tbsp vegetable oil

salt & pepper to taste

LENTILS RAGOUT

2 tbsp butter

½ cup onions

1 cloves garlic, minced

¼ cup pearl onions, peeled and roasted

¼ cup sliced pancetta, or bacon

1 cup French puy lentils

1 cup white wine

¼ cup grape or cherry tomatoes

1 tsp fresh thyme

fresh black pepper to taste

salt to taste , if required

DILL BUTTER

½ cup butter, softened

1 tbsp fresh dill, chopped

1 tbsp fresh chives, chopped

1 small shallot, chopped

1 tbsp pernod, or other anise flavored liqueur

SALMON ON LENTIL RAGOUT

Begin by soaking lentils overnight in a large bowl of cool water. This will soften them and shorten the cooking time; drain and discard the soaking liquid.

In a medium saucepot melt the butter and sauté onions, garlic and pearl onions until light brown and softened. Add drained lentils and wine and 1 cup of water, bring to a boil and reduce to a simmer; continue to cook until lentils are tender and liquid has been absorbed and reduced. Stir in tomatoes and pancetta and cook for an additional 5 minutes. Finish with herbs and pepper; taste before adding any additional salt.

Sauté shallots in a bit of butter until softened, add pernod and reduce until most of the liquid is evaporated, remove from heat and cool. Once the shallots are cooled, add to the softened butter with the herbs and combine. Season with salt and pepper to taste.

Pipe into circles or keep at room temperature until ready to serve.

Sear seasoned salmon fillets in hot oil in a non-stick pan and finish in a preheated 350°F oven for 5 minutes to finish cooking.

Serve on top of lentils and top with a spoon of herb butter.

see photo on front cover

12-16 scallops, extra large, side mussel removed

12-16 slices prosciutto, thinly sliced

12-16 leaves sage

SQUASH RISOTTO

2 tbsp butter

1 cup arborio rice

1 shallot, finely diced

½ cup white wine

6 threads saffron, (optional)

5 cups vegetable or chicken stock

½ cup grated parmesan

½ cup butternut squash, small dice

SAUCE

2 tbsp butter

2 tbsp shallots, chopped

1 tsp thyme

1 tsp tarragon

2 cups veal stock

1 cup pinot noir

salt & fresh pepper

2 tbsp butter

2 tbsp oil

PROSCIUTTO WRAPPED KING SCALLOPS ON BUTTERNUT SQUASH RISOTTO

Pat scallops dry, place 1 leaf of sage on scallop and wrap in prosciutto.

Melt butter in heavy saucepan over medium heat, add shallots and cook until transparent without color.

Add rice and coat well with butter and shallots, sauté for further 1-2 minutes. Add wine and stir until all liquid has evaporated, add stock 1 cup at a time stirring between each addition, (saffron can be added at this point), until liquid is absorbed before adding more. After you have added 3 cups of stock add squash. Cook until rice is tender but still slightly crunchy in the center. Add parmesan and adjust seasoning.

Heat butter in saucepan, sauté shallots until light brown.
Add rest of ingredients and reduce to 1 cup, adjust seasoning.

Heat butter and oil in non stick frying pan over high heat.
Place scallops in pan and cook until proscuitto starts to crisp, turn scallops over and repeat. To serve place scallops on risotto and drizzle sauce around plate.

Roasted Salmon with Prosciutto

4 portions boneless, skinless salmon

4 leaves fresh sage

4 slices prosciutto

1 tbsp olive oil

seasoning, salt & pepper

1 red onion, peeled, halved & sliced

1 lb (450 gr) fresh green beans, cleaned

2 cups baby red potatoes, cut into halves

1 cup olive oil

1 sprig rosemary

6 leaves sage

2 cups fish stock

1 cup white wine

6 tbsp butter

4 tbsp grainy mustard

2 shallots, finely chopped

ROASTED SALMON WITH PROSCIUTTO, GRAINY MUSTARD BUTTER SAUCE

In a saucepan simmer cup of olive oil, potatoes, rosemary and sage over medium until potatoes are cooked. Remove potatoes, season with salt and pepper and keep warm.

In salted boiling water blanch onion for 1 minute then refresh under cold water. Repeat for beans but boil for 4-5 minutes.

Simmer fish stock, wine and shallots down to one cup.

Remove from heat and whisk in butter until smooth, add mustard and adjust seasoning. Keep in warm place.

Place sage leaf on salmon and sear in hot pan with olive oil until brown on both sides.

Place on baking sheet with prosciutto and bake in hot oven until desired doneness is reached.

Take 2 tablespoons of olive oil from potatoes and toss onions and beans over medium heat, warming without color.

To serve, place beans, onions and potatoes in center of plate. Top with salmon and prosciutto and drizzle with sauce.

4 portions fresh tuna
1 lb (450gr) butter
2 vanilla beans, split lengthways
1 tsp sea salt

ROUILLE POTATO PURÉE
1 lb (450gr) peeled potatoes
4 cloves roasted garlic, chopped
4 tbsp butter
¼ tsp chili flakes
½ cup cream
seasoning, salt & pepper
pinch nutmeg

SAFFRON BROTH
4 cups fish stock
2 cups diced onion, carrot and celery
2 cloves garlic
2 bay leaves
½ cup tarragon
1 tsp turmeric
2 tsp olive oil
½ cup pastis or pernod

1 yellow pepper, sliced into thin strips
1 red pepper, cut into thin strips
1 bulb fennel, cut into thin strips
¼ tsp saffron threads
12 pieces jumbo shrimp, peeled & deveined
1 tbsp butter

VANILLA BUTTER POACHED AHI TUNA

Combine all ingredients together and melt over low heat, stirring occasionally. Remove from heat and let butter rest for 30 minutes, remove vanilla and scrape seeds from pods into butter, discard beans.

Boil potatoes in lots of salted water until cooked. Strain, and mash through fine sieve or ricer. Add rest of ingredients, adjust seasoning. Keep Warm.

Sauté onion, celery, carrot and garlic in olive oil until limp and without color. Add pastis, stock, turmeric, bay leaf and tarragon. Simmer until liquid has reduced by 2/3 and strain.

In a saucepan, sauté peppers and fennel with butter without color until soft. Add fish stock and saffron and bring to a simmer. Remove from heat, add shrimp and adjust seasoning.

Place tuna in vanilla butter over medium heat, making sure fish are separated and surrounded with butter. Poach for approximately 5 minutes until outer layer is seared and the inside is rare.

Remove from butter with slotted spoon and season with sea salt.

To serve, place warm potato purée in center on four large bowls. Pour saffron sauce around potato. Cut tuna in half at an angle and place on top.

see photo on page 60.

4 trout, filleted, boneless, skinless
2 tbsp butter
2 tbsp olive oil

SAUCE
½ cup butter
¼ cup olive oil
½ cup white wine
1½ tsp corn starch
juice from ½ lemon
2 tbsp chopped chives
2 tbsp chopped basil
2 tbsp chopped parsley
1 tbsp dijon mustard
salt & pepper
splash of worchester sauce

BOW RIVER TROUT FILLETS WITH CITRUS HERB SAUCE

Melt butter and olive oil together until bubbling.

Mix together wine and corn starch and whisk into simmering butter over medium heat. Continue stirring until sauce comes to a simmer, add rest of ingredients, adjust seasoning and keep warm.

To sauté trout, melt butter and oil together over medium- high heat.

Season fillets with salt and pepper and when oil is hot fry each side until light brown, then place on cloth or paper towel to remove excess oil.

To serve, ladle sauce over fish

½ cup miso paste
½ cup water
1 tbsp maple syrup
2 tbsp canola oil
1 tbsp fresh ginger, finely chopped
1 tsp garlic, finely chopped
2 tsp fresh chives

4 portions sablefish fillets
2 tbsp butter
2 tbsp canola oil
salt & pepper to taste

ROASTED SABLEFISH WITH MISO GLAZE

Miso is the paste made from fermented soya beans and comes in a variety of colors or strengths. At the hotel we use either a yellow or red paste for this recipe. This glaze tastes great with the sablefish, but is equally good with scallops or halibut.

To prepare the glaze, dissolve the miso paste in a medium bowl with warm water. Whisk in oil, maple syrup, ginger and garlic. Reserve covered in the fridge until ready to use. At this time the glaze will last up to a week refrigerated.

When cooking the fish, begin by preheating the oven to 375°F/190°C and seasoning the fillets with salt and pepper.

Heat oil in a non-stick pan, gently place the fillets in the hot oil flesh side down and cook until lightly browned, turn over and baste with glaze, being careful, as the liquid will spatter when it hits the pan. Place the fish in the oven for 10 minutes or until the fish flakes easily, add chopped chives.

Serve with steamed rice and garnish with toasted sesame seeds.

4 oz boneless, skinless halibut fillets

½ cup fava beans, blanched, peeled

½ cup snap peas, sliced

2 green onions, chopped

20 teardrop or cherry tomatoes

12 pieces white or green asparagus, peeled, half inch pieces

½ cup fresh morels

1 cup white wine

1 cup cream

1 tbsp basil, chopped

2 tbsp butter

2 tbsp oil

salt & pepper

SEARED HALIBUT ON SPRING VEGETABLES

Heat non stick frying pan over high heat,

Season halibut fillets with fresh ground pepper and a little salt.

Heat oil in pan and lightly brown fish for approximately two minutes on each side, depending on thickness.

Remove fish from pan while still medium and keep warm, fish will continue to cook for a few minutes.

Remove any excess sediment from pan then add butter, snap peas, green onion, asparagus, fava beans and morels and continue to sauté over medium heat without colour.

Add wine, cream and basil and reduce by half, add tomatoes and adjust seasoning

To serve distribute vegetables and sauce on 4 plates, place halibut on top and serve.

Braised and Roasted Back Ribs

MEAT

Beef Tenderloin

4 portions beef tenderloin

4 large scallops

PARSNIP PURÉE

2 cups parsnip, peeled & rough cut

2 cups milk

salt, pepper, nutmeg

FRICASSÉE

1 cup chanterelles

12 pearl onion, peeled

1 cup asparagus, green beans, carrot, cut into 1 inch lengths, blanched

4 baby golden beets, blanched, cut into quarters

2 tbsp butter

1 cup dark reduced stock

3 drops truffle oil

BEEF TENDERLOIN, GRILLED SCALLOP, CHANTERELLE & ROOT VEGETABLE FRICASSÉE

Simmer parsnips in milk with a pinch of salt until soft.

Blend parsnips with half of remaining milk until puréed; add more milk as required and season with salt, pepper and nutmeg. Keep warm.

In a heated pan melt butter and sauté mushrooms and onions until lightly browned, add rest of vegetables, stock and truffle oil.

Simmer until most of liquid has evaporated, adjust seasoning

Season tenderloin and scallop, grill on hot broiler until desired doneness is reached.

To serve place parsnip purée in center of plate, place beef and scallop on purée.

Spoon fricassée around edge of plate.

9 INCH PIE

This can be prepared in advance and baked just before required.

PIE PASTRY

2 cups pastry flour

7 oz (200gr) shortening or lard

1 egg

½ cup cold water

1 tbsp white vinegar

pinch salt

FILLING

12 oz (340gr) ground game meat

6 oz (170gr) ground pork shoulder

1 tbsp oil

1 chopped onion

1 stalk celery, chopped

1 cup peeled, grated potato

2 cups beef stock

1 tsp cinnamon

pinch nutmeg

½ tsp allspice

salt & fresh ground black pepper

GAME TOURTIÈRE

Place flour and salt in bowl.

Work shortening into flour until crumb texture.

Add water, beaten egg and vinegar and mix until all ingredients are combined, do not over mix.

Heat oil in heavy saucepan. Add meat, onion, celery and cook until onion starts to brown. Add rest of ingredients, stir well and continue cooking until most of liquid has evaporated.

Adjust seasoning and set aside to cool.

Preheat oven to 375°F/190°C.

Take 2/3 of pastry and roll out on floured surface. Pastry should be big enough to cover 9 inch greased pie plate.

Add meat filling, brush edge of pastry with water and cover with remaining pastry. Crimp edges of pie, beat one egg and brush over top of pie.

Sprinkle a pinch of coarse salt on pie and bake for approximately 45 minutes.

GAME HASH

4 medium yukon gold potatoes, peeled & cut in ½ inch dice, blanched

½ cup corn kernels

½ cup red onion, diced

¼ cup red peppers, diced

¼ cup cherry tomatoes, halved

2 tbsp chopped herbs, thyme, rosemary, chives, parsley

1 cup tender game meat, cut in strips or ½ inch cubes

2 tbsp oil

2 tbsp butter

½ cup game or beef stock

4 large eggs, poached

salt & fresh pepper

This dish is served at all of our lodges for breakfast, but can be served for lunch or dinner.

Season meat and sauté in a hot non stick pan or skillet with the oil until seared. Add potatoes, corn, onion and red pepper continue sautéing for a further few minutes.

Add stock, tomatoes and half of the chopped herbs reduce stock by half and add butter.

To serve place hash on large soup bowl or plate, place warm poached egg on top and sprinkle with remaining herbs.

Braised Lamb Shanks

4 lamb shanks
½ cup flour
1 tbsp paprika
1 tsp black pepper
1 tsp salt
2 tbsp vegetable oil
2 carrots, chopped
1 onion, chopped
4 stalks celery, chopped
2 tomatoes, chopped
1 orange, juiced and zest reserved
1 tbsp chopped thyme & rosemary
1 lemon, juiced and zest reserved
½ tsp caraway
½ tsp whole black peppercorns
4 cloves garlic
3 cups veal, beef or lamb stock
2 cups red wine

BRAISED LAMB SHANKS

These Alberta lamb shanks were a feature recipe on the Great Canadian Food Show when they filmed at Emerald Lake Lodge. A guaranteed crowd pleaser after a day on the ski hill, or on a chilly winter evening.

Combine flour, paprika, salt and pepper in a large plastic bag, add lamb shanks and toss them to coat evenly.

In a large saucepot heat the oil over medium heat, add lamb shanks and brown evenly, remove and set aside.

Add to the pan the vegetables and sauté until they start to brown, add tomatoes, zests, herbs and spices and sauté for 5 more minutes.

Deglaze the pot with the wine and stock and bring to a boil.

Return the shanks to the pot and reduce to a simmer, cover pot and place in oven at 350°F/180°C for approximately 2 hours or until the meat is tender. There should always be enough liquid to cover shanks so check occasionally and add stock or water as required.

Remove meat from the pot and purée the sauce until smooth, season with additional salt and pepper if needed. Place shanks back into sauce.

This dish matches well with couscous, potato purée or soft polenta.

3 cups dried penne noodles

2 cups duck confit, meat only

2 tbsp olive oil

12 roasted shallots

2 cups snap peas

1 cup fresh plums in quarters

4 tbsp basil pesto

2 cups chicken stock

½ cup plum wine

¼ cup toasted & chopped pistachio nuts

salt & pepper as required

DUCK CONFIT, PLUMS & PISTACHIO PENNE

Cook pasta in salted boiling water, strain when ready.

In a nonstick frying pan over high heat sauté shallots, plums, snap peas and duck meat in olive oil for 1 minute. Add plum wine, pesto and stock and simmer for 1 minute.

Add noodles and sauté all ingredients together until well combined, adjust seasoning and divide onto 4 plates.

5 lbs (2.2KG) baby back pork ribs

MARINADE

¼ cup concentrate orange juice

2 cups rice wine vinegar

2 cups honey

¼ cup sesame seed oil

1 tbsp chopped fresh ginger

½ cup chopped green onions

½ cup diced red onion

½ cup soy sauce

2 tbsp chopped garlic

1 tbsp chopped basil and oregano

1 tbsp ground black pepper

1 orange cut into thin slices

CILANTRO'S BARBEQUED PORK RIBS

Combine all ingredients together and massage into ribs. Marinate for 2 days in refrigerator, turning occasionally.

Cook ribs over low heat on barbecue, brushing with marinade until ribs are cooked.

1 lamb leg with bone removed, (your butcher can do this) trimmed of most fat

2 sprigs each of rosemary, thyme, oregano, mint

4 bay leaves

1 tbsp crushed peppercorns

1 clove garlic, crushed

¼ cup olive oil

juice & zest from 1 lemon

2 cups white wine

6 cups beef or lamb stock

1 carrot diced

1 onion diced

HERB ROASTED LAMB LEG WITH PAN JUICES

Combine ingredients on the top part of the list and rub into Lamb. Place in container, cover and refrigerate overnight. Remove meat from fridge 1 hour before you intend to start cooking.

Preheat roasting pan in 400°F/200°C oven. Season lamb with salt. Place lamb in roasting pan and sear for 5 minutes, then turn over, continue roasting for a further 20 minutes. Turn leg over again and add vegetables, after 10 minutes, add wine and stock. Continue roasting for a further 15 minutes or until internal temperature reaches 130°F. For medium-rare, cooking time will depend on size of leg.

Remove lamb from pan when desired doneness is reached and let rest for at least 10 minutes before carving.

You will require 2 cups of pan juices so you may need to reduce liquid or add water. Strain remaining juices through fine sieve and adjust seasoning.

Serve with risotto and your favorite vegetables.

Roast Elk Tenderloin

1 ½ lb (680gr) elk tenderloin (can be substituted with either venison or beef)

SAUCE

3 cups reduced game or beef stock

½ cup red wine

½ cup port wine

2 tbsp butter

1 tsp crushed juniper berries

1 tbsp chopped shallots

2 tbsp rosehip jelly.

salt & pepper

SQUASH HASH

2 cups butternut squash, peeled, ½ inch dice

½ cup pearl onions

½ cup fresh chanterelles

½ cup teardrop tomatoes, halved

1 tbsp chopped chives & thyme

2 tbsp butter

1 tbsp oil

salt & pepper

ROAST ELK TENDERLOIN, SQUASH HASH & WILD ROSE GAME REDUCTION

Served at the James Beard House in New York

In a saucepan melt butter and sauté shallots and juniper until light brown, add red wine, port and stock.

Simmer stock and reduce by two thirds. Pass through fine sieve, add jelly and continue cooking until sauce starts to thicken, Adjust seasoning and keep warm.

Season tenderloin with salt and pepper and sear in hot frying pan, place in 425°F/220°C oven for 12-15 minutes for medium rare cooking. Remove tenderloin and let rest for ten minutes before cutting.

Sauté squash in butter and oil until it starts to brown slightly. Add onions and chanterelles and continue for further 4-5 minutes, drain any excess fat, add seasoning and herbs.

To assemble place potato hash in center of plate arrange sliced tenderloin against hash and drizzle sauce around edge of plate.

8-12 meaty back ribs, (cilantro uses elk ribs)

1 tbsp oil

seasoning, salt & pepper

6 cups beef stock

MARINADE

1 tsp garlic, minced

1 chipotle chili, chopped

6 tbsp rosehip jelly

½ cup oyster sauce

¼ cup soya sauce

1 tsp ground black pepper

2 tbsp oil

SAUCE

½ cup rosehip jelly

1 tbsp ancho chili puree

1 tbsp orange juice concentrate

1 tbsp water

BRAISED & ROASTED BACK RIBS

Season ribs and sear in hot pan until brown.

Place in a baking pan or ovenware pot with stock, cover and braise at 350°F/180°C for 2 hours.

Remove ribs from stock and strain any remaining liquid.

Combine all marinade ingredients together with ribs and braising liquid.

Return to baking pan, cover and continue cooking for further 1-2 hours at 250°F/160°C or until meat starts to fall from the bone.

Stir occasionally.

Bring all sauce ingredients to a simmer and strain.

To serve place ribs in hot oven on a baking tray and roast until dark brown, serve on sauce.

see photo on page 72

CREAMED YOUNG CHICKEN COCOTTE

2 whole young chicken

2 cups porcini mushrooms, sliced (can be substituted with button mushrooms)

6 cloves roasted garlic

2 shallots sliced

1 sprig fresh thyme

2 tbsp olive oil

¼ cup white wine

½ cup chicken stock

1 ½ cups whipping cream

salt & pepper

Quarter whole chickens and dry completely. Heat oil in sauté pan and brown skin on chicken, remove chicken and set aside.

Add mushrooms, garlic and shallots and lightly brown. Add white wine, chicken stock and cream. Bring to a simmer and season.

Place chicken and sauce into heavy ovenproof casserole with a tight fitting lid and cook in preheated oven 375°F/190°C for 30-40 minutes.

VENISON RAGOUT

1 ½ lb (680gr) venison stew meat, cut into 1 inch dice

2 tbsp oil

2 onions cut into fine dice

1 cup mixed sliced mushrooms

1 cup red wine

2 tbsp red currant jelly

2 tbsp tomato paste

1 tbsp paprika

1 tsp crushed juniper

1 orange, juice and zest

1 tbsp fresh thyme

1 tbsp worcestershire sauce

salt & fresh ground pepper

Season meat and sauté with a little oil in heavy saucepan until it starts to brown. Add onions and mushrooms and continue cooking until onion are limp.

Add rest of ingredients and heat until stew comes to a simmer. Simmer over medium heat for approximately 1 hour or until meat is tender. Add water as needed, there should be just enough sauce to cover meat.

Adjust seasoning and serve with gnocchi or spaetzli and braised red cabbage.

4 rib-eye steaks

CHIPOTLE SAUCE
1 cup cranberry juice
14 oz (400gr) pear compote with juice
14 oz (400ml) apple juice
½ cup apple cider vinegar
1 tsp thyme
2-3 smoked chipotle peppers
2 cups veal glaze

MEXICAN SLAW
1 cup shredded Jicama
½ cup shredded carrot
½ cup shredded zucchini
½ cup shredded red/yellow pepper
¼ cup olive oil
1 lemon & lime, zest & juice
1 orange zest & lime
¼ cup rice wine vinegar
½ tsp red pepper flakes
salt & pepper to season

CHEESE ENCHILADAS
½ cup grated havarti cheese
½ cup grated smoked gouda
½ cup grated asiago
¼ cup chopped green onion
1 tsp black pepper
chilli flakes to taste
4 x 8 inch tortillas

BUFFALO RIB-EYE STEAK, SMOKED CHIPOTLE SAUCE, MEXICAN SLAW & FRIED ENCHILADA

For the sauce, bring all ingredients to a boil and simmer for 20 minutes.

Purée until smooth and pass through sieve. Heat sauce as required.

For the Mexican slaw, combine all ingredients together and adjust seasoning.

Combine all ingredients for the enchiladas,

4 x 8 inch flour tortillas. Brush tortillas with olive oil, divide cheese mix between tortillas and roll tightly. Seal ends with flour and water mix.

To serve, season steaks with salt and fresh pepper, cook on hot grill until required temperature is reached, let meat rest for 5 minutes before serving.

Heat enchiladas on top of grill until brown and cheese is melting.

Place sauce on warm plate, put steak on sauce. Arrange slaw and enchiladas around steak and serve.

MEATBALLS

1 lb (450gr) medium ground beef

1 tbsp prepared hot horseradish

2 tbsp dijon mustard

½ cup onion, finely chopped

2 cloves garlic, minced

1 tbsp worcestershire sauce

seasoning, salt & fresh ground black pepper

SAUCE

1 tbsp butter

1 tbsp oil

1 portabella mushroom, skin & gills removed, small diced

1 shallot, small dice

¼ cup red wine

1 cup reduced veal glaze

seasoning

ALBERTA BEEF MEATBALLS

Combine all ingredients together and form into approximately 10 balls.

Place balls on a baking tray and bake in preheated oven 425°F/220°C for 10-12 minutes.

Over medium heat sauté diced mushroom and shallot in butter and oil until lightly browned.

Add wine and stock and reduce to approximately ½ cup.

Serve meatballs and sauce together and garnish with fresh shaved parmesan.

Tamarind Glazed Duck Breast

4 duck breasts, trimmed & skin scored

MARINADE

1 can coconut milk

1 tsp turmeric

1 tsp chili powder

1 tsp honey

½ tsp tamarind concentrate

1 shallot, diced

1 tsp chopped ginger

DATE ORANGE CHUTNEY

2 oranges, juice from both & zest from one

1 cup dates chopped

1 tsp sugar

1 tsp chopped shallots

TAMARIND GLAZED DUCK BREAST WITH DATE & ORANGE CHUTNEY

Combine all ingredients for the marinade together and pour over duck breasts, cover and refrigerate for up to 6 hours.

Combine all ingredients together and simmer over medium heat. When liquid has almost evaporated remove from heat and allow to cool.

Remove duck breast from marinade season with salt and pepper and place skin down on preheated non stick pan over medium high heat. Sear duck until it reaches a deep brown color, then flip breasts over and place in preheated oven 400°F/200°F for 5 minutes.

Remove duck from pan and allow to rest for 5 minutes. Place date chutney into pan with 1 tablespoon of sauterne jelly and 1 cup of game glaze or beef stock. Reduce sauce until it thickens.

Slice duck and serve on sauce.

Osso Buco

OSSO BUCO

4 x 1 ½ inch thick slices of venison, beef, veal or pork shank

1 tbsp flour

1 tbsp paprika

salt & fresh ground pepper

½ cup oil

2 cups chopped carrot, celery & onion

1 clove garlic

2 bay leafs

½ cup fresh herbs, rosemary, thyme & basil

½ tsp caraway

zest from 1 lemon

2 cups red wine

4 cups meat stock

4 large tomatoes, chopped

salt & fresh ground pepper

Mix flour and paprika together.

Heat oil in heavy ovenware pan.

Season shanks and dredge in flour mix. Brown on both sides and remove from pan.

Add carrot, celery, onion and garlic to pan used to sear shanks, sauté over medium heat until vegetables start to brown, drain excess fat..

Add rest of ingredients and bring to a simmer.

Add seared shanks to simmering stock.

Place covered pan in preheated oven 375°F/190°C for 3-4 hours, check occasionally and add water if needed so that meat is always covered in liquid.

When meat can easily falls from the bone remove shanks from sauce.

Blend sauce and pass through a strainer onto shanks.

Bring to a simmer and adjust seasoning. Serve.

4 x portions Buffalo Tenderloin
(Meat in this recipe can be substituted with other game meat or beef)

BRAISED RIBS
4 buffalo short ribs
4 tbsp oil
1 onion diced
1 carrot diced
1 stalk celery diced
2 tomatoes, chopped
2 tbsp tomato paste
2 bay leaves
4 sprig of fresh thyme
1 cup red wine
4 cups beef or game stock
seasoning, salt & pepper

SAUCE
½ cup morel mushrooms, rinsed & cleaned
2 tbls butter
1 tsp fine chopped shallots
1 cup reduced sauce from ribs
½ cup red wine
salt & pepper

BUFFALO TENDERLOIN ON BUFFALO SHORT RIB, YAM & PEARL ONION HASH WITH MOREL SAUCE

First prepare ribs as this takes from 1-2 hours to cook.
Trim excess fat from spare ribs and season with salt and pepper.

Heat heavy pan over medium heat. Sear ribs until brown on all sides, add vegetables and continue browning, add tomato paste and brown for a further few minutes. Add wine, stock, thyme and bay leaf.

Place lid on pan and simmer or place in preheated oven 300°F/150°C until meat starts to fall off of bone.

Add stock or water if required. Remove meat from sauce and let cool.

Strain sauce and skim excess fat, reduce until sauce starts to thicken, this will be the base for the morel sauce.

To make sauce sauté morels and shallots in butter until light brown. Add wine and sauce from ribs, reduce until desired thickness is reached, adjust seasoning and keep warm.

Season tenderloin and start to cook on well heated grill. We recommend that prime cuts of game meat are not cooked over medium rare for optimal flavour and texture.

YAM HASH

2 cups quarter inch dice yam, blanched

½ cup pearl onions, cleaned

2 tbsp sundried cherries or blueberries

1 tbsp chopped herbs, parsley, thyme, chive

¼ cup game or beef stock

1 tbsp butter

1 tbsp olive oil

salt & pepper

While meat is cooking prepare Yam hash.

Heat nonstick frying pan.

Cut meat away from spare rib bones and course dice, discard bones.

Add oil and butter to pan and sauté pearl onions until light brown, Add yams, berries, stock, seasoning and herbs.

Continue cooking until all ingredients are hot and stock has evaporated.

Before serving it is best to let tenderloin rest for a few minutes to continue cooking through.

To serve place hash in center of plate, place tenderloin on hash then drizzle sauce around meat.

White Wine Chicken with Pancetta

4 chicken breasts, skin on

2 tbls olive oil

1 cup button mushrooms, quartered

½ cup pearl onions, peeled

½ cup pancetta, cut into strips

1 cup white wine

2 cups chicken stock

1 tbsp butter

2 tbsp fresh chives, chopped

salt & pepper to taste

WHITE WINE CHICKEN WITH PANCETTA

To prepare this dish, heat oil in an oven safe pan and place the seasoned chicken breast into the pan skin side down and cook until the skin is browned. Turn over and lightly brown other side, add the quartered mushrooms, onions and pancetta and cook for further 2-3 minutes. Add the white wine and stock and bring to a simmer, place the pan in a 375°F/190°C oven and bake for 15 minutes. The chicken will feel firm to the touch and the liquid will be reduced to about one third.

Remove the chicken from the pan and place on the serving dish; place the saucepan back onto the stove and bring the remaining liquid to a simmer, add a little water if necessary to de-glaze the pan.

Simmer and stir in the butter and chives, do not boil at this point or the butter will separate from the stock. Season if necessary with salt and pepper, tasting first as the pancetta may be salty.

Pour the sauce over the chicken and enjoy.

At the lodge we serve this dish with potato gnocchi that we bake along with the chicken. The gnocchi can be made a day in advance and bake at the same time as the chicken.

STARCHES
& SIDES

2 tbsp dry mustard
¼ cup yellow mustard seeds
¼ cup water
2 tbsp dried blueberries
2 tbsp white wine
½ cup apple cider vinegar
1 clove garlic
1 tbsp brown sugar
½ tsp salt
¼ tsp ground allspice
¼ tsp ground ginger

BLUEBERRY MUSTARD

This is a lovely game meat condiment, and is great on a sandwich although a rather startling purple color.

In a small bowl, whisk together the water, wine, mustards and blueberries and set aside to rehydrate.

In a saucepot combine the remaining ingredients and bring to a boil, reduce to a simmer and continue to cook for 5 minutes.

Whisk the mustard mixture into the vinegar and simmer for an additional 10 minutes. Remove from the heat and cover and sit for 3 hours, these allow the seeds and berries to soften and the flavors to meld together.

Pulse a couple of time with either a hand blender or in a blender to break up the seeds and berries. Store covered in the refrigerator for up to a week.

½ cup onion, fine diced
2 cloves garlic, minced
2 tbsp duck fat
½ cup carrots, fine diced
1 cup french puy lentils
2 cups poultry stock
1 tomato, diced
1 cup duck confit meat
1 tsp fresh thyme, chopped
1 tsp fresh oregano, chopped
salt & fresh ground pepper

LENTIL, DUCK CONFIT RAGOUT

This recipe calls for both duck confit and duck fat. If you don't want to include all those extra steps and time, substitute half the amount of duck confit with a good quality smoked bacon and sauté before starting the recipe. Use the rendered bacon fat in place of the duck fat.

Begin by soaking lentils overnight in a large bowl of cool water. This will soften them and shorten the cooking time; drain and discard the soaking liquid.

In a medium saucepot melt the duck fat and sauté onions, garlic and carrots until light brown and softened.

Add drained lentils and stock, bring to a boil and reduce to a simmer; continue to cook until lentils are tender and stock has been absorbed and reduced, water may need to be added.

Stir in tomatoes and confit and cook for an additional 5 minutes.

Finish with herbs and pepper; taste before adding any addition salt.

Cranberry Relish

CRANBERRY CHUTNEY

1 cup sugar
3 cups cranberries
1 cup dried cranberries
½ cup orange juice
1 orange zest and juice
1 cinnamon stick
1 tbsp ground black pepper
1 tbsp fresh ginger, finely chopped
1 cup red wine
1 tsp salt

Combine all ingredients in stock pot and simmer, stir regularly.

Cook until liquid has consistency of jam.

Great with any poultry dish, hot or cold.

CRANBERRY RELISH

2 cups dried cranberries
2 cups dried cherries
½ cup sundried tomatoes
½ cup diced red onion
2 tbsp shallots, fine diced
1 cup water
½ cup port
1 1/3 cups balsamic vinegar
1 1/3 cups brown sugar
¾ cups red wine
1 tsp fresh ground black pepper

Simmer all ingredients over medium heat until liquid starts to thicken and coat fruit.

Store in refrigerator in sealed container and use as required.

Complements all cold cuts and cured meats.

1 cup half & half cream

1 cup whipping cream

¼ cup chantrelles (dry)

1 bay leaf

1 tbsp butter

1½ cups assorted mushrooms

2 tsp shallots

1 tsp garlic

2 whole eggs

1 egg yolk

1½ cups bread, brioche or country loaf

1 tbsp fresh thyme

salt & pepper

MUSHROOM BREAD PUDDING

Preheat oven to 350°F/180C and lightly butter a 2 liter casserole dish and set aside.

To prepare the bread, cut into 1 inch squares and set aside until custard is ready. It is perfectly fine if the bread is stale or dries out as this just increases the custard that it will absorb. Place the bread in a bowl large enough to easily mix the bread and custard.

For the custard, in a sauce pot bring to a simmer the creams, dried mushrooms and the bay leaf. Simmer for 10 minutes or until the mushrooms are tender, remove from heat and cool slightly. Slice mushrooms into bite sized pieces and sauté with the butter, garlic and shallots; cooking until lightly browned and all the extra moisture is evaporated and add to the bread.

When the cream is cooled slightly add the lightly beaten eggs and yolk and pour onto the bread and mushroom mix, gently stir everything together to coat, the mixture may be soft. Pour into the prepared casserole dish and cover with foil.

Place the casserole into a water bath, a baking pan with hot water about 1 inch deep, and into the oven 350F/180C for 30 minutes. The casserole will be set, but still very moist.

This can also be made into individual puddings, divide mix into four ramekins and decrease baking time to only 15 minutes.

1 cup white beans

1 onion, diced

1 tbsp garlic, minced

1 tbsp canola oil

½ cup pancetta, small cubes

¼ cup double smoked bacon, small cubes

1 tbsp fresh sage

4 cups chicken stock

½ cup cherry tomatoes, halved

2 tbsp mollases

1 tbsp maple syrup

2 tbsp tomato paste

salt & pepper

EMERALD LAKE PORK & BEANS

The beans are best made the day before and allowed to mellow and reheated the next day when you cook the pork.

Place in beans into a container and cover with water and soak overnight, adding water if necessary to keep them covered.

The next day, sauté the onions and garlic until transparent in a medium saucepot, add the drained beans and cover with the stock.

Bring to a boil and reduce to a simmer, cooking until the beans are tender; if they start to stick to the bottom of the pot before they are cooked add extra stock or water.

When the beans are tender most of the water should be absorbed, but if there is still a lot of water in them, continue to cook and reduce the liquid until it just coats the bottom of the pot.

While the beans are cooking, fry the cubes of pancetta and bacon until fat has been rendered then drain on paper towel.

Add meat and rest of ingredients to the beans, mix thoroughly and continue cooking until desired thickness is reached.

Adjust seasoning.

2 nectarines

2 plum

½ cup red onion, finely diced

1 tbsp white sugar

3 tbsp raspberry vinegar

2 tbsp oil

¼ cup red currant jelly

2 star anise

1 cinnamon stick

salt & pepper

NECTARINE & PLUM COMPOTE

Peel and seed fruit, cut into thin slices. Heat oil over medium heat, add onion and sauté without color.

Add rest of ingredients and simmer until most of the liquid has evaporated, adjust seasoning, remove cinnamon stick and star anise.

Serve at room temperature.

2 cups all purpose flour

2 eggs

¾ cup milk

2 tbsp grainy mustard

1 tsp salt

pinch nutmeg, fresh ground pepper

GRAINY MUSTARD SPAETZLE

Combine eggs, milk and mustard together in mixing bowl. Slowly beat in flour and salt until a smooth batter is achieved. Over boiling and salted water push batter through a pasta colander. When spaetzle reaches a rolling boil and is floating it is ready. Strain spaetzle and rinse under cold water to refresh.

If you are not using immediately oil lightly and place in sealed container and refrigerate.

To serve melt 2 tablespoons butter in nonstick frying pan over medium heat, add spaetzle and toss until noodles are hot.

Adjust seasoning and serve.

1 cup sugar
½ cup water
1 cup white vinegar
2 tbsp dry mustard
2 cantaloupe melons

MUSTARD MELONS

Peel and seed the melons and cut into 1 inch (2cm) chunks and place in a no-reactive bowl or container.

In a small bowl combine sugar, mustard, water and vinegar, pour over the melon chunks, cover and place in the refrigerator for 1 to 2 days, stirring once or twice.

After the melons have marinated, place them and the liquid into a heavy bottomed saucepot and slowly bring up to a simmer.

Continue to cook slowly over low heat until the syrup is clear and the melons are translucent.

Remove the melon pieces with a slotted spoon and set aside in a clean dish.

Continue reducing mustard liquid until it starts to slightly thicken.

Pour liquid over melon in sterilized container, store in refrigerator for up to one month.

These melons are great with all cold cuts and cured meats. Finely chopped they also combine well in a vinaigrette.

ONION MARMALADE

2 white onion, peeled, finely sliced
2 red onions, peeled, finely sliced
¼ cup shallots, finely sliced
2 tbsp olive oil
1 tbsp fresh thyme, chopped
1 cup brown sugar
1 cup white wine
¼ cup balsamic vinegar
½ cup marmalade jam
1 tsp ground black pepper
salt

Simmer onions and shallots in olive oil until lightly brown, add rest of ingredients and continue cooking until nearly all of liquid has evaporated.

This matches well with all grilled meats, and especially adds flavor to sandwiches.

RED CHILI SALSA

6 ripe tomatoes, cut in half
1 cup tomatillos, leaves removed
1 small white onion, cut in half
2 garlic cloves
2 cascabel chilies, seeded
2 arbol chilies
1 serrano chili, seeded
2 tbsp olive oil
1 tsp salt
1 tsp sugar

Toss all ingredients together and place on a baking tray. Place in a preheated oven at 425°F/220°C for 10 minutes.

Cool slightly then coarse chop in food processor.

Place ingredients in a sauce pot and simmer for 2 minutes.

Cool and use as required

1 lb (450gr) sweet potato, peeled, thinly sliced

½ lb (225gr) potato, peeled, thinly sliced

2 tbsp soft goat cheese

½ cup leek, thinly sliced

1 cup half & half cream

½ cup whipping cream

1 tsp fresh thyme, chopped

1 tbsp butter

salt & pepper, to taste

pinch nutmeg

SWEET POTATO & GOAT CHEESE GRATIN

Preheat the oven to 350°F/180°C and lightly butter a loaf pan lined with parchment paper. The parchment isn't necessary, but it will make the gratin a lot easier to remove from the pan, if you don't have any just butter the pan a little more generously.

In a large bowl combine all of the ingredients together. Mix thoroughly until all the potatoes are evenly coated with cream.

Pack the potatoes evenly into the prepared loaf pan.

Place in the oven and cook for 1 hour or until the potatoes are tender, cover with foil when potatoes are golden brown.

Remove from the oven and allow to cool for 20-30 minutes before inverting onto a serving tray.

This can also be made in a casserole dish and served directly from the dish at the table.

SQUASH RISOTTO

2 tbsp butter

1 cup arborio rice

1 shallot, finely diced

½ cup white wine

6 threads saffron, (optional)

5 cups vegetable or chicken stock

½ cup grated parmesan

½ cup butternut squash, small dice

Melt butter in heavy saucepan over medium heat, add shallots and cook until transparent without colour. Add rice and coat well with butter and shallots, sauté for further 1-2 minutes.

Add wine and stir until all liquid has evaporated, add stock 1 cup at a time stirring between each addition, (saffron can be added at this point) until liquid is absorbed before adding more.

After you have added 3 cups of stock add squash. Cook until rice is tender but still slightly crunchy in the center. Add parmesan and adjust seasoning.

TROPICAL SALSA

l cup ripe mango, cut into small dice

1 cup papaya, cut into small dice

1 cup pineapple cut into mall dice

2 tbsp chopped cilantro

2 tbsp red onion, fine diced

½ tsp salt

½ tsp pepper

¼ tsp chili flakes

1 tsp sugar

1 lemon, zest & juice

1 orange, zest & juice

1 lime, zest & juice

Combine all ingredients and let rest for one hour before using, adjust seasoning.

This salsa works well with fish and poultry.

1 ¼ lbs (560gr) yukon gold potatoes

2 eggs

½ tsp ground nutmeg

½ cup flour

1 tsp salt

½ tsp pepper

POTATO GNOCCHI

Preheat the oven to 400°F and place the washed and pricked potatoes in and bake for 1 hour or until flesh is tender.

Remove from the oven and cut in half, scoop the potato flesh into a bowl while still very hot and mash trying to get rid of as many lumps as possible. If you have a potato ricer, that works great but isn't necessary. Into the hot potatoes add the seasoning, flour and lightly beaten eggs and mix everything to combine. Turn potato mix onto a flour dusted counter top and knead lightly about 10 times, adding a little extra flour if necessary. Divide dough into half and roll into snakes about 2cm in diameter cut into pieces 2 cm long and roll in lightly in flour.

Bring a large pot of water to a boil and gently place to gnocchi in, a few at a time and returning the pot to a low boil and cook until the gnocchi float on the top, remove and cool in a bowl of ice water. Continue to cook in batches and cooling. Remove from the ice water and drain, the gnocchi can be made in advance and kept in the refrigerator.

Banana Trio

SWEETS

1.8 cups flour
½ cup brown sugar
½ tbsp ground cinnamon
¾ tsp baking powder
¾ tsp baking soda
½ tsp ground allspice
½ tsp ground ginger
¾ cup shortening
¾ cup molasses
¾ cup water
1 ½ eggs

SPICE SYRUP

1 ½ cups water
1 ½ cups sugar
1 cinnamon stick
1 tsp allspice
3 star anise
1 tsp grated fresh ginger

GINGERBREAD SYRUP CAKES

Combine all dry ingredients and mix briefly with paddle in mixing bowl.

Slowly add shortening and continue mixing until it reaches a crumb texture.

Add molasses, eggs, water and continue mixing until smooth. Grease a muffin pan with shortening and ¾ fill each unit with cake mixture.

Bake at 375°F/190°C for 25 minutes.

Bring all ingredients for the syrup to a boil and reduce to simmer for 5 minutes. Remove from heat and rest for 30 minutes. Strain through fine sieve.

Unmold gingerbread cakes while still warm and drizzle 2 oz syrup on each cake.

Cakes can be served immediately or wrapped in cling film and refrigerated then microwave for 30 seconds before serving.

Serves with caramelized apples or pears and your favorite ice cream.

3 ½ cups flour

½ tsp baking soda

1 tsp baking powder

¼ tsp ground cinnamon

¼ tsp salt

4 eggs

1 cup ground hazelnuts

1 tbsp vanilla extract

1 cup sliced blanched almonds

6 oz (190gr) almond paste, room temperature

½ cup butter, room temperature

2 cups sugar

ALMOND HAZELNUT BISCOTTI

In a mixing bowl combine flour, baking soda, baking powder, cinnamon and salt.

In another mixing bowl beat the almond paste and sugar together, add butter and mix until creamy. Add hazelnuts, eggs and vanilla.

Fold into flour until completely combined. Add almonds.

Divide dough into three and mold into loaves approximately 10 inches long on a baking sheet.

Bake for 35 minutes at 375°F/190°C.

Let biscotti rest for 20 minutes then remove from baking sheet and place on cutting board.

Slice biscotti approximately half inch thick, then place individual biscotti flat onto baking sheet to semi dry overnight.

Store in airtight container.

Lemon Tart

TART PASTRY

10 oz (300 gr) butter
6 ½ oz (180 gr) icing sugar
1 ½ oz (40 gr) egg white
3 ½ oz (100 gr) egg yolk
20 oz (570 gr) pastry flour

LEMON FILLING

4 ½ oz (130 gr) fresh lemon juice
2 lemons, zest only
5 oz (140 gr) sugar
4 oz (110 gr) butter
4 eggs

LEMON TART

Beat together butter and sugar in mixing bowl until creamy and smooth, approximately 5 minutes.

Slowly add egg yolks then egg whites until well blended. Add flour in three batches and combine into mixture, do not over mix.

Wrap in cling film and refrigerate for a least 2 hours.

Roll pastry out to 1/4 inch thick and mold into your tart shells.

Rest pastry for 15 minutes then blind bake (place foil then rice or dried beans for weight) for 12 minutes at 350°F/180°C.

Remove weight and foil and continue baking for approximately 5 minutes until pastry is light brown.

Place all ingredients in steel bowl over boiling water. Whisk frequently until mixture is combined and thickened.

Transfer to a new bowl, cover with cling film and cool.

Spoon lemon curd into cooked tart shell filling almost to rim then smooth out flat.

Finish by sprinkling 1 tablespoon of sugar evenly over tart and caramelize with blow torch.

Serve with fresh berries and your favorite sorbet.

PEAR CAKE

4 cups flour

2 cups sugar

3 tsp baking soda

1 tsp salt

9 eggs

1½ cups canola oil

2 cups grated pear

1 cup grated apple

PUMPKIN MARMALADE

1 ½ cups pumpkin, small dice

2/3 cup sugar

1 orange, zest and juice

pinch allspice

pinch cinnamon

½ cup apple juice

BERRY REDUCTION

2 cups saskatoon berries

1 cup blueberries

1 cup port

3 tbsp honey

PEAR & GOAT CHEESE CAKE

Preheat oven to 350°F/180°C.

Whip oil, eggs and sugar together. Fold in rest of ingredients and bake on greased cookie sheet for 25-30 minutes.

Simmer all ingredients for the marmalade together until pumpkin is soft and liquid has evaporated, you may need to add water during cooking if pumpkin is not yet soft.

Mash pumpkin with a fork leaving small pieces of pumpkin. Set aside.

Process berries through a juicer, discard pulp.

Combine berry juice with port and honey and reduce liquid over medium heat.

Continue cooking until juice starts to reduce and thicken slightly, strain and cool to room temperature.

CHEESE CAKE

6 oz (170gr) cream cheese

12 oz (340gr) goat cheese

½ cup mascarpone cheese

½ cup suger, powdered

1 orange, zest and juice

1 tbsp vanilla extract

½ cup cream, whipped firm

Beat cheeses, sugar, juice and vanilla together until well combined. Fold in cream and mix until smooth..

Cut cake into 6 individual size forms or 1 spring form. Spread pumpkin over sponge then top with cheese mix. Place in fridge and let set.

To serve place cheese cake in center of plate and drizzle berry reduction around plate.

Garnish with dried pear or sprig of mint.

1 cup carrots, peeled and grated

1 cup zucchini, washed and grated

1 lb (450gr) sugar

5 oz (145ml) vegetable oil

5 eggs

2 tbsp baking soda

1 ¼ lb (570gr) all purpose flour

6 oz (170gr) sour cream

1 tsp salt

CARROT & ZUCCHINI BREAD

Combine sugar, oil and eggs together in mixing bowl. Add rest of ingredients and mix until well combined.

Grease 2 x 2 lb loaf pans. Divide mix evenly between both pans.

Place in preheated oven 375°F/190°C for 45 minutes.

Let loaves cool for 30 minutes then turn out onto a cooling rack.

HEALTH COOKIES

1 cup butter

1 cup brown sugar

pinch of salt

¼ cup corn syrup

2 eggs

1 tsp vanilla

3 cups rolled oats

2 tbls maple syrup

½ cup sunflower seeds

1 cup coconut

3 apples, grated or finely diced

½ dried cherries, chopped

½ cup flour

1 ½ cups chocolate chips

¼ cup poppy seeds

½ cup almonds

2 cups rice krispies

Preheat oven to 350°F and grease 2 cookie sheets or line with parchment paper and set aside.

Mix together the butter and sugar until fluffy, add the eggs and beat until light , add the syrups and salt and combine thoroughly.

Mix together all the dry ingredients except the krispies and slowly mix into the egg mix.

Mix in the diced apples and krispies at the very end, mixing only until combined.

Place ¼ cup scoops onto a greased cookie sheet and bake for 20 minutes.

5 cups whole oats
1 cup sliced almonds
½ cup brown sugar
1 tbsp cinnamon
½ tsp nutmeg
1 orange, zest only
1/3 cup sunflower seeds

10 oz (300gr) butter, melted
½ cup maple syrup
¼ cup canola oil

½ cup shredded coconut, toasted
¾ cup raisins
¼ cup dried cranberries

GRANOLA

Combine first set of ingredients together.

Add butter, maple syrup and oil to dry ingredients and toss together until well mixed.

Spread out on baking sheet and roast in preheated oven 375°F/190°C for approximately 15 minutes or until granola is golden brown.

Sprinkle the shredded coconut, raisins and cranberries over the granola.

Place on rack and allow to cool.

Granola will need to be broken up into bite size pieces and stored in air tight container.

Vanilla Cheese Cake

VANILLA CHEESE CAKE

CRUST

2 cups graham crumbs

½ cup sugar

3 ½ oz (100gr) melted butter

FILLING

1 lb (450gr) cream cheese, room temperature

5 oz (140gr) sour cream

5 oz (140gr) sugar

2 tbsp corn starch

4 small eggs

2 vanilla bean, split in half & scrape seeds from bean

Combine all ingredients for the crust together and press a quarter inch thick into prepared mold or cake form.

Bake in preheated oven 325°F/160°C for 10 minutes.

Mix together cream cheese and vanilla seeds. Add sour cream and mix well.

Add sugar and corn starch and mix, slowly add eggs and beat until smooth.

Pour over precooked base and place in oven at 250°F/130°C for 40 minutes. When cooled serve with seasonal berries or ice cream.

BANANA BREAD

18 oz (510gr) banana, mashed

18 oz (510gr) brown sugar

1 cup vegetable oil

3 eggs

1 tbsp baking soda

17 oz all purpose flour

¾ cup milk

pinch of salt

MAKES 2 LOAVES

Combine sugar, oil and eggs together in mixing bowl. Add rest of ingredients and mix until well combined.

Grease 2 x 2 lb loaf pans. Divide banana mix evenly between both pans.

Place in preheated oven 375°F/190°C for 45 minutes. Let loaves cool for 30 minutes then turn out onto a cooling rack.

This bread can be eaten as is or also makes great French toast for breakfast.

CHOCOLATE HAZELNUT PASTE

10 oz (280 gr) soft butter

5 oz (140 gr) icing sugar

2 eggs

¼ cup ground hazelnuts

½ cup cocoa powder

¼ tsp salt

15 oz (425 gr) pastry flour

BAKED CHERRY & CHOCOLATE TART

Cream together in mixer butter and icing sugar. Slowly incorporate eggs.

Sift cocoa into flour, add salt and hazelnuts then slowly add to butter, do not over mix.

Wrap pastry in cling film and refrigerate for at least 2 hours.

Roll pastry out to 1/4 inch thick and mold into your tart shells.

Blind bake pastry (place foil then rice or dried beans for weight) and bake for 10 minutes at 350°F/180°C.

Remove weight and bake for further 4 minutes.

Place chocolate, butter and zest in steel bowl and melt over boiling water, remove from heat and set aside.

Whisk eggs, yolks and sugar in steel bowl over simmering water until mixture is warm to touch.

Transfer to electric mixer and whisk until mixture starts to cool and doubles in volume.

Fold chocolate into egg mixture.

CHERRY CHOCOLATE FILLING

10 oz (280 gr) semisweet chocolate

5 oz (140 gr)butter

2 oranges, zest only

2 eggs

2 oz (55 gr) egg yolks

2 oz (55 gr) sugar

1 cup pitted cherries

MAKES 4 X 6 INCH TARTS

Place enough cherries in tart shell to cover bottom.

Spoon chocolate mixture over cherries until covered, smooth out level.

Bake for 12 minutes at 275°F/140°C.

Let rest for 30 minutes, unmold and serve with caramel ice cream or mascarpone.

Fallen Chocolate Soufflé

10 oz (280gr) semi sweet chocolate

3 oz (85gr) unsalted butter

1 orange, zested

3 egg whites

1 tbsp corn starch

pinch salt

FALLEN CHOCOLATE SOUFFLÉ

Melt chocolate, butter and zest in double boiler.

Remove and cool to room temperature.

Whisk egg whites and salt together and beat until stiff peaks are formed but still moist.

Fold egg whites and corn starch into chocolate then half fill greased ramekin molds or individual cake rings.

Bake at 375°F/190°C for 10 minutes and allow to cool slightly before serving.

Serve with ice cream, fresh berries or espresso anglaise.

Chocolatissimo

CAKE

5 oz (145gr) dark chocolate

5 oz (145gr) butter

3 ½ oz (100gr) sugar

2 egg yolks

3 eggs

2 tbsp strong espresso coffee

CHOCOLATE FILLING

9 ½ oz (270gr) semisweet chocolate

7 ½ oz (200gr) cereal cream

14 oz (400gr) whipping cream

1 tsp gelatin, or 1 leaf

CAKE ICING

5 oz (145gr) semisweet chocolate, chopped

5 oz (145gr) whipping cream

1 oz (30gr) sugar

CHOCOLATISSIMO

Melt chocolate and butter together over double boiler.

Whisk eggs, yolks and sugar until light and fluffy. Fold chocolate and eggs together with espresso.

Pour evenly into 2 prepared cake tins and bake at 325°F/160°C for 20 minutes. Cakes will fall when removed from oven, allow to cool.

Heat cereal cream to tepid and dissolve gelatin in cream. Add cereal cream to chocolate and melt over double boiler.

Allow chocolate mix to cool below room temperature until almost starting to set.

Whisk whipping cream until it starts to thicken, fold into chocolate. Divide chocolate into two and pour one onto cake base in a spring form pan.

Add another base onto filling then pour second filling and top with remaining base to create 2 layers of chocolate. Allow cake to cool.

Bring cream and sugar to a boil. Pour over chopped chocolate and stir until smooth.

Place in fridge and stir frequently until cool to touch.

Pour slowly over cooled cake and place in fridge until it sets.

1 pint fresh strawberries, cleaned & quartered

½ cup late harvest wine

2 tbsp fireweed honey

1 tbsp sugar

1 orange, zest only

SABAYON

6 egg yolks

½ cup sugar

1 cup whipping cream

FIREWEED HONEY & ICE WINE SABAYON OVER MARINATED STRAWBERRIES

Combine wine, sugar and honey together and heat to room temperature.

Pour over strawberries, add zest and marinate for 1 hour.

Drain liquid from strawberries and set aside.

Whisk egg yolks and sugar in stainless steel bowl over simmering water until mixture doubles in volume.

Add liquid set aside from strawberries and continue whisking over simmering water until sabayon thickens, whisking vigorously. Place sabayon over ice and carefully fold mixture until it starts to cool.

Whisk whipping cream until stiff and fold into cooling sabayon.

Divide strawberries equally into four serving coups or martini glasses and pour sabayon over strawberries.

Chill for at least 1 hour and serve.

GANACHE CENTER

2 ½ oz (70ml) cream

3 oz (85gr) semi sweet chocolate (melted)

1 tbsp grand marnier

CAKE BATTER

6 oz (170gr) semi sweet chocolate

5 ½ oz (160gr) unsalted butter

5 ½ oz (160gr) sugar

2 ½ oz (70gr) cake flour

5 eggs

CHOCOLATE MOLTEN CAKE

Bring cream to boiling point and pour over melted chocolate, mix well until smooth. Add Grand Marnier and stir until combined. Pour into an ice cube tray and refrigerate until solid.

Melt chocolate and butter together in a double boiler, remove when smooth and cool to room temperature.

Whisk eggs and sugar together and combine with chocolate and butter.

Fold in sifted flour, cover and place in refrigerator overnight. Spoon mixture into 4-6 non stick ramekins or baking rings to ¾ full.

Place ganache cube into center of batter. Bake in preheated oven 375°F/190°C for 10-12 minutes until cakes harden slightly and rise around edges.

Remove from oven and allow to cool slightly for 30 minutes. Serve with you favorite ice cream.

Cakes can also be refrigerated and reheated in warm oven or microwave.

BUMBLEBERRY PIE

PASTRY

3 cups flour

pinch salt

1 cup shortening or lard, cut into cubes

6 tbsp cold water

1 egg

1 tsp white vinegar

FILLING

2 apples, peeled, cored and diced

1 cup rhubarb, chopped

1 cup raspberries

½ cup blueberries

1 cup blackberries

1 cup strawberries

1 cup sugar

1 tbsp corn starch

1 tbsp flour

1 tbsp lemon juice

Crumble flour and shortening together, do not over mix.

Add rest of ingredients and mix until all ingredients are combined and hold together be careful not to over mix. Wrap in cling film and let rest for 1 hour.

Combine all ingredients for the filling together.

Divide pastry in two with one having slightly more dough than the other.

Roll out larger portion of dough a little larger that the pie shell. Place dough in well greased pie plate. Fill pie plate with pie filling.

Roll our remaining dough; dampen edges of pastry with a little water and place over pie shell, crimping together edges with other pastry.

Brush top of pie with a little water or egg wash, sprinkle coarse sugar over pie,

Put a small cut in center of pie and bake in preheated oven 350°F/180°C for approximately 45 minutes, or until pie is golden brown and ingredients are bubbling.

1 cup blackberries
1 cup sour cherries
1 cup cranberries
1 cup strawberries
1 cup blueberries
1 cup raspberries
1 cup rhubarb
4 cups sugar
2 tbsp lemon juice
1 tbsp salt

BUMBLEBERRY JAM

Combine all ingredients together and marinate overnight in cool area.

In a heavy bottom sauce pan bring berries to a rolling simmer over medium heat.

Continue cooking stirring frequently until jam starts to thicken. You can test consistency of jam by placing a teaspoonful on a small plate and placing it in the refrigerator until it cools.

When jam has reached desired consistency you can preserved in sterilized jars.

Pour jam almost to top of jars, seal with lid and place in boiling water for 10 minutes to complete preserving.

Double Chocolate Kahlua Pate

WHITE CHOCOLATE PATE

7 oz (200gr) white chocolate, coarse chopped

7 oz (200ml) cream, semi whipped

3 oz (85gr) butter at room temperature

2 tbsp icing sugar

DARK PATE

1 cup butter at room temperature

4 ½ oz (130gr) icing sugar

5 oz (140gr) dark chocolate

3 oz (85ml) kahlua

4 oz (115gr) cocoa powder, sifted

2 cups cream, semi whipped

½ cup pasteurized egg yolks

¼ oz (7gr) gelatine sheets soaked in cold water

DOUBLE CHOCOLATE KAHLUA PATE

Place white chocolate in steel bowl and melt over simmering water. Whisk together butter and icing sugar in mixer.

Slowly pour just tepid melted chocolate into butter mixture until well combined. Gently fold in semi whipped cream and set aside.

Place dark chocolate in steel bowl and melt over simmering water. Whisk together butter and icing sugar in mixer. Add alternately cocoa and eggs into butter and mix until smooth.

Heat kahlua and add softened gelatine, remove from heat and stir until dissolved. Add kahlua to butter mixture.

Slowly add just tepid melted chocolate until combined, mixture may appear grainy. Fold in semi whipped cream until combined.

To construct pate, line pate mold or loaf tin with cling film.

When chocolate mixes are almost starting to set alternate ½ inch layers of white and dark chocolate until mixture are all used.

Place in fridge and let set for minimum of four hours.

Unmold from cling film and place on solid flat surface.

To serve, warm a knife under hot water and slice ¼ inch piece from pate and place on plate, garnish with fruit purees and fresh berries.

SUPER MOIST BANANA CAKE

¼ loaf banana bread, (see recipe) diced into cubes

4 ½ oz (125ml) cereal cream

2 eggs

1 tbsp sugar

1 orange, zested

1 ripe banana, sliced

CARAMEL POPCORN BRITTLE

½ cup popped corn

¼ cup butter

¾ cup white sugar

¼ cup corn syrup

½ tsp salt

¼ tsp baking soda

½ cup roasted peanuts, chopped

PEANUT BUTTER MOUSSE

4 oz (110gr) cream cheese

1 ½ oz (40gr) sour cream

2 tbsp sugar

3 oz (85gr) peanut butter

½ cup of whipping cream

BANANA CAKE WITH BANANA NAPOLEON & POPCORN BRITTLE

Bring to a boil cream, sugar and zest. Remove from heat and whisk in eggs, pass through a strainer over banana bread and mash together with ripe banana until smooth.

Pour into pre greased muffin molds, and bake at 320°F/160°C for 15 minutes, they should be firm to touch.

Place in sealed container until ready to use.

Melt butter in saucepan, add sugar and corn syrup, boil for 8-10 minutes over medium heat until light brown.

Remove from heat and carefully stir in salt and baking soda, immediately add popcorn and peanuts.

Spread onto foil lined tray and place in preheated oven 300F/150C for 25-30 minutes.

Remove from oven and before brittle completely hardens break off portion size pieces.

Keep at room temperature.

For the caramelized banana cut a banana into 2 inch long by ¼ inch thick strips.

CHOCOLATE MOUSSE

4 ¼ oz (125gr) dark chocolate

5 oz (140gr) whipping cream, whisked until stiff

1 egg yolk

½ egg

1 tbsp sugar

Place on nonstick baking tray and sprinkle with white sugar.

Place under broiler until sugar has melted and caramelized, repeat process to obtain thicker caramel.

You will require 3 pieces for each napoleon.

For the peanut butter mousse, combine peanut butter, cream cheese, sour cream and sugar until smooth. Whisk whipping cream and fold into peanut butter mixture.

For the chocolate mousse, whisk egg yolk, egg and sugar over double boiler until creamy then remove from heat and continue whisking until it reaches room temperature.

Melt chocolate and fold into egg mix. Fold in whipped cream.

To assemble pipe alternate layers on chocolate and peanut butter mousse between caramelized bananas. .

Heat banana pudding briefly in microwave or oven

Place popcorn brittle on chocolate mousse, with cake and napoleon.

see photo on page 110

Top: Emerald Lake Lodge. *Left:* Sunrise at Emerald Lake. *Center:* Emerald Lake Lodge ca.1905. *Right:* Chef Morrison in the herb garden.

EMERALD LAKE LODGE

History

Emerald Lake Lodge has been a popular destination for savvy travellers since its construction in 1902 by the Canadian Pacific Railway.

Perched on the edge of Emerald Lake's impossibly turquoise waters (near Field, B.C.), the hand-hewn timber cabin seduced guests with its unforgettable vistas of prime Canadian wilderness.

From its earliest days, access into the heart of Yoho National Park (Yoho means "to be in awe of" in Cree) and the park's world-class hiking trails have been key to the lodge's popularity.

In fact, the encouragement of internationally renowned English mountaineer Edward Whymper is what reportedly convinced CP management to build on the site in the first place.

Although its rooms back then were modest, the lodge — referred to in its early days as Emerald Lake Chalet — housed an elegant dining room which became an instant hit with well-heeled guests arriving on foot or by horseback.

Under the eventual ownership of the Smyth family, followed by the Holschers, and, finally, the O'Connors (current owners since 1979), Emerald Lake Lodge has remained true to its roots.

Cilantro at Emerald Lake Lodge.

Connie O'Connor says she and her husband Pat take tremendous pride in showcasing the historic property not only to Canadians but to visitors from around the globe.

"When the lodge was run by CP, no one was going to Emerald Lake unless they were high up in society or with the railroad," she explains.

"We've tried to make it accessible to everyone. This perfectly pristine valley speaks to a hundred years of people coming to enjoy the mountains. The area is the same — regardless if you came today or back in 1902."

Yoho Lounge.

Left: Kicking Horse Lounge. *Right:* Cabin entrance mid-winter.

Concept

When the O'Connors purchased Emerald Lake Lodge in 1979 the accommodations had only been open to the public during the summer season.

"We couldn't understand this," recalls Pat. "Of course, the summer is beautiful, but winter is incredible, too. We wanted to open year round."

Winter transforms the lodge and the forests surrounding it into a picture-perfect wonderland.

Proximity to local ski resorts in nearby Lake Louise and Golden makes the lodge an obvious ski holiday destination. The potential for skating and cross-country skiing on and around the frozen lake is an additional draw.

"We wanted the property to be a high-end resort," continues Pat, adding that in the early 1980's there was public demand for more sophisticated accommodations in the national parks.

"We wanted to create a distinct architectural look by retaining historical elements while creating a high-end but casual atmosphere."

The couple also envisioned a lodge that would service not just those interested in climbing local peaks, but also those, no matter what their age or background, who were searching for a tranquil refuge away from city life.

"Obviously, if you're a super athlete, it's great. You can climb Mount Burgess, hike to Takakkaw Falls, and there are scrambles to Emerald Peak. But it's a playground for whatever your level," says Connie, who is an avid climber herself.

"But a simple walk down by the lake will give you a peace and serenity you're not ever going to find in a city.

"I have always believed the mountains are for everyone."

Atmosphere

Today, after years of renovations, construction and fine-tuning, what makes Emerald Lake Lodge so attractive to visitors is its mix of that which is civilized and that which is wild.

Picture the elegant, outdoor hot tub overlooking the jade waters of a glacier-fed lake. Imagine sitting down to dinner with a bottle of fine wine and locally inspired cuisine after an exhilarating day skiing in the Rockies.

"Emerald Lake Lodge is a marriage of everything. The fire is crackling. There are the forests and the mountains. There is no stress or pressure," says Alistair Barnes, executive chef of Canadian Rocky Mountain Resorts.

"And you're sitting down to a beautiful plate of something like slowly braised short ribs topped with a tenderloin of elk with rose-hip glaze."

In other words, few would dispute the O'Connor's success in marrying a luxury experience with some of the most impressive wilderness Canada has to offer.

Still, says Connie, she and her husband are always upgrading the lodge's atmosphere. The lodge already boasts private rooms with wood-burning fireplaces and bed covers as soft as velvet.

"I'm always playing with fabrics and searching out comfortable

Summer pathways.

Cilantro on the lake.

furniture," she says. "I suppose the best compliment I get is when guests are about to leave and they say 'I wish I had booked in longer.'"

If anyone is equipped to judge the lodge's transformation from rustic cabin to luxury lodge, it would be Bob Sandford, author of *Emerald Lake Lodge: A History and A Celebration.*

"While Emerald Lake Lodge was once a rough and ready retreat beckoning adventurers into the heart of the Rockies, it has been transformed in our time into something grander," observes the historian.

Fire pit overlooking the lake.

Top: Deer Lodge at Lake Louise. *Left:* Mount Fairview dining room. *Center:* Patio. *Right:* Tower room.

DEER LODGE

History

Originally built around 1911, Deer Lodge, with its hand-hewn timber design, represents to this day the classic definition of rustic mountain accommodations.

"People visited in the summers and when you came you were made to feel like you weren't just a visitor, but that you were part of a family," says historian Bob Sandford of the lodge which is located minutes by foot from from Lake Louise, Canada's most celebrated Rocky Mountain lake.

Pat and Connie O'Connor purchased the property from the estate of George O. Brewster and Crosby Company Limited in 1982; four years later, the newly renovated building welcomed visitors year round.

"Once we were committed to the mountains and the opportunity came up to purchase Deer Lodge, to purchase this little jewel just steps away from one of the planet's most beautiful views," recalls Connie, "we thought 'Oh God, now this is an opportunity!'"

Concept

When the O'Connors bought Deer Lodge, their goal was to provide the public with a cozy, family oriented mountain experience.

"But one with exquisite dining," adds Connie. "We've always had a strong emphasis, with all of our properties, on food."

According to Pat, the lodge serves two markets: international tourism during the summer months and a local clientele during the ski season.

"Deer Lodge has the convenience of a world-class ski hill only five minutes away," he says. What's more, the lodge features a lively après ski atmosphere featuring a rooftop hot tub with an incredible view of Mount Fairview and the Victoria glacier.

Sitting room.

Atmosphere

One of the most striking qualities of Deer Lodge today is the serenity of the location.

Despite its proximity to Lake Louise, which draws continuous traffic from Banff National Park during the summer, the historic lodge is a sanctuary.

"You'll see people writing in their journals and reading the paper. It's peaceful and quiet and yet they're five minutes from the lake front and nearby [Fairmont hotel] where it's a zoo," says Connie.

Connie says she often has to reassure repeat guests that she will not change a thing about Deer Lodge. They appreciate how the property retains that "I'm back. I've gone back in time and I'm in the mountains" feeling.

While many properties in the mountains are going down the luxury accommodation route, says Sandford, Deer Lodge remains small and intimately connected to a sense of place.

"I think the O'Connors want to be seen as people who have made a commitment to the lodge's original qualities, enduring qualities of the experience of place rather than luxury for luxury's sake. This approach appeals to a certain sophisticated element of the travelling public."

Top: Buffalo Mountain Lodge. *Left:* Hot tub. *Center:* Sleeping Buffalo dining room. *Right:* Bird bath.

BUFFALO MOUNTAIN LODGE

History

Pat and Connie O'Connor couldn't resist purchasing Banff's Mountview Village when the opportunity arose in 1987.

Not only was the property minutes from the town centre, but Banff National Park — the glorious mountain playground that it is — has been an international tourist destination since its establishment in 1885.

The couple saw huge potential in the motel whose management, at the time, rented modest cabins to skiers in search of lodging during the winter months.

"It made sense to Pat to have something in Banff. It was a beautiful, under-developed property on a hill overlooking Rundle Mountain and the Bow Valley," recalls Connie.

The hill to which she is referring was named Tunnel Mountain by the Canadian Pacific Railway, but it was originally called "Sleeping Buffalo Mountain" by First Nations people in the area because of its likeness to a giant, slumbering buffalo.

On April 20, 1988, the O'Connors changed the name of their latest acquisition to Buffalo Mountain Lodge as a nod of respect to local native traditions. "The First Nations were here way before the Canadian Pacific Railway," says Connie. "I have a lot of respect for their history."

Top: Wapiti Longhouse Conference Center. *Left:* Wapiti Longhouse.
Right: Wine room.

143

Buffalo Mountain Lodge premier king room.

Concept

According to the O'Connors, by the late 1980s Calgarians were beginning to demand higher-end accommodations in the nearby mountain town of Banff.

"We needed to get away from the cookie-cutter hotels that line Banff Avenue. So we aimed for a smallsized luxury resort with fine dining," says Connie. "We saw a niche for both city slickers — who want a comfortable mountain experience — and those who are true mountain people."

Still, the couple wanted to interweave native history and culture throughout the mountain getaway.

"We built the Wapiti Long House," Connie continues, going on to explain that "wapiti" means "elk" in Shawnee.

"Plus, we feature a number of native artifacts. One of the highlights is a ceremonial dress that was a gift to Pat's grandmother from the local native community. She was committed to the education of their women," says Connie.

Buffalo Mountain Lodge opened formally on the night of March 26, 1988. "It was one of the biggest snow storms of the year. Alistair worked his magic and we served a whole hip of tasty buffalo," remembers Connie.

Cilantro, Banff.

144

Atmosphere

Today, Buffalo Mountain Lodge — an hour and 15 minutes by car from Calgary — encapsulates the O'Connor's mountain property vision; in other words, it's a place where leisure meets luxury.

"This is what we've aspired to," says Connie. "We avoid being pretentious but we want to provide an intimate, luxury experience. We're truly a boutique hotel."

Popular as a corporate retreat as well as a wedding and honeymoon destination, the lodge is meticulously maintained; its grounds and colourful gardens leave a lasting impression. Deer can often be seen enjoying the plants during the summer months, quietly nibbling on flowers early in the morning. Elk, cougars and bears frequent the Banff area, too.

The rooms are decorated in a warm, inviting style. The cozy beds are bedecked in silky smooth fabrics and the stylish bathrooms feature oversized claw-foot tubs. The main lodge is built in an open post and beam style fitting for a mountain retreat, and a gorgeous fieldstone fireplace in the lounge beckons visitors to its hearth no matter what the season.

Sleeping Buffalo, the lodge's main dining room, features a sophisticated menu with everything from tender CRMR farm-raised game to mouthwatering Alberta

Festive season.

Winter at the Lodge.

lamb. Another dining option includes the more rustic Cilantro Mountain Café which features flat-crust pizzas cooked in a wood-burning oven.

"Our dishes are pretty exciting. Even our game burgers, for example, are served with Alistair's special relish," muses Connie.

"I want people to leave the lodge (and all our properties) having experienced the mountains which I have great passion for. I want them to have had a delicious, indigenous meal that they likely would never have prepared at home."

The invitation to the 1988 launch of Buffalo Mountain Lodge included a quote that sums up the couple's respect for mountain life. The quote, from Chief John Snow of the Stoney Indian Band, read:

"These mountains are our temples, our sanctuaries and our resting places. They are a place of hope, a place of vision, a place of refuge, a very special and holy place where the Great Spirit speaks with us. These mountains are our sacred places."

Cilantro main dining room.

CILANTRO

History

Cilantro was one of the first restaurants in Calgary to break the steakhouse mould by introducing the city to Californian-Southwestern cuisine and it is as popular and welcoming today as it was 20 years ago when the doors were first opened.

The building was originally a men's tailor shop with the suits and fabrics occupying the front of the store and the tailoring/residence located in the back. Since then, the space has had a colourful history having hosted the likes of blues man Jeff Healy and impromptu poetry readings under the guise of Marty's Café.

Concept

When California was forming the nucleus of its modern food identity it looked to its neighbours to the south and southwest, in many ways a logical progression. It was a bold step for Cilantro to go down this road in the 1980s, but it was clearly the right step; the distinctive flavours of the southwest are deftly incorporated into the restaurants ever-changing menu with impressive results.

The adobe wood-burning oven turns out some of the best pizza in town and the wine list is diverse and well balanced. Game meats from our Ranch are also an important fixture on the menu, providing diners with healthy and delicious alternatives to the usual carnivorous fare.

Atmosphere

Cilantro offers a warm and inviting space to dine, a room that could best be described as casual elegance personified. The historic charm of the one-time residence has been preserved, yet the room feels contemporary and spacious.

One of Cilantro's most endearing features is its patio, an oasis amid the hustle and flow of Calgary's 17th Avenue. The vine-covered walls and mature trees provide an idyllic backdrop for diners when the weather cooperates, and when it doesn't there is the warmth of the wood-burning oven to take the chill off. The back bar affords patrons a great place to mingle and after spending an hour or so there you might even pick up a few tips on the art of pizza making, Cal-Ital style.

These are just a few of the reasons why Cilantro remains a perennial favourite amid Calgary's burgeoning dining scene.

Cilantro lounge.

Top: Divino bar. *Left:* Divino Bistro. *Center:* Chef John Donovan. *Right:* Stephen Avenue entrance.

DIVINO

History

Many seasoned diners recall Divino Bistro when it opened back in 1984 as a quaint 30-seat restaurant in the the iconic Grain Exchange Building. Nearly two decades later, the bistro's new owners — Canadian Rocky Mountain Resorts — established a new location two blocks away. Contributing to the city's exciting rejuvenation of Stephen Avenue Walk (8th Avenue), Divino Wine & Cheese Bistro opened its doors in 2003 in the historic Calgary Wine & Spirits Building. The name proudly remained the same, but patrons soon discovered that the modernized Divino Bistro was simply "bigger and better".

Stone wine cellar.

Concept

The owners of Canadian Rocky Mountain Resorts, Pat and Connie O'Connor, have long admired the traditional bistros that have thrived for decades throughout New York City. With this concept in mind, the modern décor of Divino was infused with a comforting bistro atmosphere. The same wood-burning grill found at the famous Gramercy Tavern in New York City was incorporated into the restaurant. With its extensive cheese and wine selection, Divino has successfully transplanted the distinctive American bistro style into western Canada.

Divino Wine & Cheese Bistro typically seats 100 people each day during the energetic lunch hour and the same again in the evening. But there is more to Divino than meets the eye. Catering to both social and corporate clients, Divino Bistro offers two private rooms in which to host cocktail parties, corporate meetings and intimate dinners — it is a three-floor restaurant to suit a wide variety of needs.

Divino is committed to supporting local artists and artisans, and their works can be found on the restaurant's brick walls. This commitment is extended to the menu as well, with the inclusion of seasonal ingredients from local producers.

Atmosphere

When you step into Divino your senses are immediately alerted to subtle notes of charred applewood backed by the cacophony of bistro bustle. Divino's open kitchen design not only adds atmosphere and warmth to the room, but also serves as a culinary "workshop" for those who are afforded a view along the lengthy red leather banquette.

To compliment the bistro fare created by the talented group of chefs, there is an impressive cheese display flanking the kitchen, a temptation that many find hard to resist.

With an award-winning wine program that features over 500 international labels, Divino's educated staff will always find that perfect glass of wine to complement your evening. If this is your draw to the restaurant, join the other wine-loving patrons who line the bar, and explore the many libations that the bistro has to offer. Come and see for yourself why Divino Wine & Cheese Bistro continues to be one of downtown Calgary's most successful restaurants.

Velvet at the Grand.

VELVET

History

The historic Lougheed Building in downtown Calgary that Velvet calls home was built in 1912 and has survived a fire and a few close encounters with the wrecking ball. Happily, it survives and is close to being completely restored to its original glory.

The building was home to the Grand Theatre, a storied venue that had been graced by such latter-day luminaries as Paul Robeson, Fred Astaire, Tyrone Power Sr. and Sarah Bernhardt, to name but a few. The catwalks that have been cleverly integrated into Velvet's ceiling were rescued from the original theatre and one can only imagine the tales they could tell if they could talk.

Concept

Velvet is the newest member to the CRMR group, a striking departure in concept and design from the company's other properties. Velvet enjoys a symbiotic relationship with The Grand, home to Theatre Junction and their cutting edge production company. In many ways, the new theatre is retracing the steps of its glorious past by presenting some of the most original works and artists working today.

Velvet is the ideal spot for a pre-show dinner or, if you opt for after-the-show drinks, you may rub shoulders with the artists who kept you entertained that evening. Rumour has it, artists have been known to enjoy a cocktail or two.

Atmosphere

Neon cool meets the urban theatre scene in Velvet and while it may look like a hip nightclub, the focus remains on great food served in an inviting atmosphere. Downtown Calgary has shed its cow town image and Velvet reflects that fact in its unique interior, a space that looks as if it were lifted right out of Manhattan or London.

Dining room.

Historic Lougheed building.

151

Top: The Ranche. *Left:* Charlie's lounge. *Center:* Formal room. *Right:* Parlour.

THE RANCHE

History

This stately manor was originally built for William Roper Hull in 1896, a cattle baron and developer who left a significant footprint on Calgary's landscape. He enlisted renowned Calgary architect James Llewellyn Wilson to design the building which would he would eventually call the Bow Valley Ranche. It is located in what is now known as Fish Creek Provincial Park (Canada's largest urban park) on the southern edge of the city, an area rich in natural beauty that is teeming with wildlife.

The property was sold to senator Patrick Burns in 1902 and remained with his family until 1969. It was then sold to the province in 1973 and was left boarded up until the efforts of a small but dedicated group of individuals helped bring it back to life. Two of the areas local residents — Mitzie and Larry Wasyliw — persuaded local MLA Heather Forsyth to help them form The Ranche at Fish Creek Society. The group managed to raise $100,000 in private donations, enough to get the restoration started. Calgary restaurateur Witold Twardowski was also instrumental in restoring the building to what it is today — a charming restaurant that serves as a grand testament to an era gone by.

Grand salon.

Concept

It took the dedication and hard work of many individuals to get The Ranche to where it is today, but in the end it was the considerable resources and management skills of the CRMR team that put the project on solid ground. The Ranche's main dining room operates on a daily basis while the various function rooms and idyllic grounds host countless weddings and corporate events throughout the year. Fish Creek Park offers myriad pathways ideally suited to walking and cycling, a perfect prelude to lunch or dinner at The Ranche.

Atmosphere

As you pass through the white picket fence gate and head up the cobblestone walk to the main entrance of The Ranche the sense of history is palpable. The main-floor dining room is a grand space framed by a massive wood-burning fireplace, a warm and inviting space to wine, dine and unwind. The Ranche is a unique place that offers respite from the bustle of city life, a restaurant where old world charm goes hand in hand with contemporary food to create an unforgettable dining experience.

153

Top: Grazing Buffalo. *Left:* Free ranging Elk. *Center:* Brad O'Connor and Dr. Terry Church. *Right:* Prairie winter.

THE FARM

History

In 1996 the O'Connor family founded Canadian Rocky Mountain Ranch as a source for wholesome, high quality game meats for their group of restaurants and resorts. Brad O'Connor oversees the operation, which is situated on 540 acres of pristine Alberta foothills. Issues such as breeding stock, land costs and fencing made this an expensive undertaking but it has proven to be immensely successful and the family now distributes the meat between their restaurants and numerous wholesalers across the province. Dr Terry Church – one of Canada's leading livestock experts – was enlisted to insure that the herds remained healthy and that the conditions were ideal for them to thrive. He now resides on the ranch and his expertise has proved invaluable.

Concept

Game meat was initially a little slow to catch on, perhaps because most people had initially experienced it through the efforts of hunters who would distribute their take among friends and family. The gamey taste typically associated with wild meat is very different from the farm-raised animals for a number of reasons. On the ranch the feed is controlled and the product is processed at a federally inspected and approved facility. In many ways it offers the best of both worlds as it is a naturally raised product but is free from the hormones and steroids that are turning so many consumers away from commercially processed beef. Above all though it is the taste that has won most people over, both our elk and buffalo have been huge hits in our restaurants and the demand has now spread throughout the retail sector. The meat is also very lean but flavour is not sacrificed by the lack of "marbling" as it is with beef. Customers in both Alberta and B.C. can now order the product on-line at www.crmranch.com

Top: Painted Boat Resort. *Left:* THE RESTAURANT, pool and marina at sunset. *Right:* THE RESTAURANT patio.

PAINTED BOAT

History

Painted Boat Resort, Spa and Marina is Canadian Rocky Mountain Resorts' first property on British Columbia's Sunshine Coast. From Vancouver it is a 40 minute ferry ride out of Horseshoe Bay, and is approximately a 50 minute drive along the beautiful winding road to Pender Harbour.

The resort was originally known as the very popular Lowe's Resort built in 1952. The traditional family-run resort was a draw to local families and yearly returning guests interested in fishing, kayaking, boating or just hoping to relax and unwind on the marina's beach front.

Taking its new name from the vibrant old fishing crafts that traveled the waters of the Strait, Painted Boat pays tribute to the location's past while celebrating the future.

Resort master bedroom and ensuite.

Concept

Half a century later, Lowe's Resort has been transformed into a luxurious Oceanside resort offering quality accommodations and services to those who are attracted to the area's natural grandeur.

Nestled amongst five acres of Douglas fir, red cedar and arbutus trees, the 31 waterfront vacation villas offer spectacular water views and large balconies complete with BBQs. Inspired by the fishing structures along the coastline, Painted Boat has a distinctly 'west coast' look and feel, evoked through the use of exposed timber construction and expansive windows. The extensive use of natural materials blends seamlessly with the forested setting.

Quarter condo ownership is the prime attraction for the area and CRMR is the managing company for the rental side of the resort.

Lavishly furnished, with an emphasis on comfort, the enormous two-bedroom suites offer fully-equipped open kitchens, including granite countertops, stainless steel appliances and west facing ocean views.

Atmosphere

THE RESTAURANT at Painted Boat is the newest addition to Canadian Rocky Mountain Resorts' family of award-winning restaurants. Perched over calming waters overlooking the stunning marina, this 70 seat contemporary bistro offers a mixture of bamboo, metal and local art giving a very distinct modern coastal feel.

Open year round, THE RESTAURANT eagerly focuses on the abundance of fresh, local ingredients helping us create a vibrant and approachable regional menu.

THE RESTAURANT also offers clients the ability to book a private second-floor room for business or family events. This room is ideal for inspiring corporate meetings, weddings or festive cocktail parties, which may spill out onto the private west facing sun deck.

The resort's philosophy is simple: leave as small a footprint as possible and let the natural features of the area shine through. Where the bald eagles fly above and the sea otters play below this resort is known for its peaceful serenity. Once you experience this four-season resort, you will truly never leave.

BIN 905

Concept

Bin 905 was established in 1997 to serve Calgary's growing thirst for premium wines and spirits. The restaurants and resorts within the CRMR group naturally benefit from the wealth of knowledge that has become synonymous with Bin 905; most of the staff are either certified sommeliers or sommeliers in training. The management team at Bin 905 travels the world in search of unique and sought-after wines, many of which are exclusive to the CRMR group. Visitors constantly re

mark that the selection and serviceoffered at Bin 905 are unmatched in the Canadian market, and that is certainly one of the store's goals. They offer a series of provocative and unique in-store wine tastings throughout the year in the laid-back confines of the tasting room. The store provides a unique shopping experience with something for every budget and taste.

The Globe and Mail called Bin 905 the "best place in Canada to find rare wine".

Published by TouchWood Editions, 2008
Originally published by Altitude Publishing Canada Ltd., 2007

Text, recipes and photographs copyright © 2007 Canadian Rocky Mountain Resorts

Extreme care has been taken to ensure that all information presented in this book is accurate and up to date.

TouchWood Editions
108 – 17665 66A Avenue
Surrey, BC V3S 2A7
www.touchwoodeditions.com

TouchWood Editions
PO Box 468
Custer, WA
98240-0468

LIBRARY AND ARCHIVES CANADA CATALOGUING IN PUBLICATION

Barnes, Alistair, 1956-
Simple treasures : from the collection of Canadian Rocky Mountain resorts / Alistair Barnes.

Includes index.
ISBN 978-1-894898-85-0

1. Cookery. 2. Resorts--Rocky Mountains, Canadian (B.C. and Alta.).
3. Restaurants--Rocky Mountains, Canadian (B.C. and Alta.). I. Title.

TX715.6.B37 2008   641.5   C2008-906359-7

Library of Congress Control Number: 2008937298

TouchWood Editions acknowledges the financial support for its publishing program from the Government of Canada through the Book Publishing Industry Development Program (BPIDP), Canada Council for the Arts, and the province of British Columbia through the British Columbia Arts Council and the Book Publishing Tax Credit.

Printed in Canada

Canadian Rocky Mountain Resorts wish to acknowledge the writers and photographers who helped create this book.

Writers: Kim Gray, Jamie Bryshun, Alistair Barnes, Patrick and Constance O'Connor, Geoff Last

Photographers: Brian Buchsdruecker, Bookstrucker Photography, Food Photographs, Colin Smith, Jason Dziver, Robert Lemermeyer